JOSEPH BRODSKY, winn... ...., ...

in Literature, was born in 1940 in Leningrad. He came
to the United States in 1972 as an involuntary exile from
the Soviet Union. He served as U.S. Poet Laureate in
1991 and 1992. His publications include *On Grief and
Reason*, a collection of essays, and *So Forth*, a book of
poems. He died in January 1996.

SEAMUS HEANEY, who was awarded the 1995 Nobel
Prize in Literature, was born in 1939 in County Derry,
Ireland. He has published many books of poetry and
criticism, most recently *The Spirit Level* and *The Redress
of Poetry*. A resident of Dublin, he spends part of each
year teaching at Harvard University, where he is the
Boylston Professor of Rhetoric and Oratory.

DEREK WALCOTT, winner of the 1992 Nobel Prize
in Literature, was born in St. Lucia in 1930. His works
include *Omeros*, *The Arkansas Testament*, *Collected
Poems: 1948–1984*, and his newest, *The Bounty*. He lives
in New York City and Castries, St. Lucia.

HOMAGE TO

ROBERT FROST

HOMAGE TO

ROBERT FROST

JOSEPH BRODSKY

SEAMUS HEANEY

DEREK WALCOTT

THE NOONDAY PRESS

FARRAR STRAUS GIROUX .

NEW YORK

The Noonday Press
A division of Farrar, Straus and Giroux
19 Union Square West, New York 10003

These three essays have also appeared in the following publications:
"On Grief and Reason": The New Yorker, 1994, and On Grief and Reason by
Joseph Brodsky © 1995 by Joseph Brodsky; "Above the Brim: On Robert Frost":
Salmagundi #88–89; "The Road Taken": The New Republic.

The Library of Congress has catalogued the hardcover edition as follows:
Brodsky, Joseph, 1940–
    Homage to Frost / Joseph Brodsky, Seamus Heaney, Derek Walcott.
    p.   cm.
    ISBN 0-374-14814-7 (alk. paper)
    1. Frost, Robert, 1874–1963—Criticism and interpretation.
I. Heaney, Seamus. II. Walcott, Derek. III.Title.
PS3511.R94Z5557   1996
811'.52—dc20   96-15655

CONTENTS

JOSEPH BRODSKY

On Grief and Reason

Robert Frost using his homemade writing board, Franconia,
New Hampshire, 1915. (Courtesy of Herbert H. Lamson Library,
Plymouth State College, Plymouth, N.H.)

I

I should tell you that what follows is a spinoff of a seminar given four years ago at the Collège International de Philosophie, in Paris. Hence a certain breeziness to the pace; hence, too, the paucity of biographical material—irrelevant, in my view, to the analysis of a work of art in general, and particularly where a foreign audience is concerned. In any case, the pronoun "you" in these pages stands for those ignorant of or poorly acquainted with the lyrical and narrative strengths of the poetry of Robert Frost. But, first, some basics.

Robert Frost was born in 1874 and died in 1963, at the age of eighty-eight. One marriage, six children; fairly strapped when young; farming, and, later, teaching jobs in various schools. Not much traveling until late in his life; he mostly resided on the East Coast, in New England. If biography accounts for poetry, this one should have resulted in none. Yet he published nine books of poems; the second one, *North of Boston*, which came out when he was forty, made him famous. That was in 1914.

After that, his sailing was a bit smoother. But literary fame is not exactly popularity. As it happens, it took the Second World War to bring Frost's work to the general public's notice. In 1943, the Council on Books in Wartime distributed fifty thousand copies of Frost's "Come In" to United States troops stationed overseas, as a morale-builder. By 1955, his *Selected Poems* was in its fourth edition, and one could speak of his poetry's having acquired national standing.

It did. In the course of nearly five decades following the publication of *North of Boston*, Frost reaped every possible reward and honor an American poet can get; shortly before Frost's death, John Kennedy invited him to read a poem at the Inauguration ceremony. Along with recognition naturally came a great deal of envy and resentment, a substantial contribution to which emerged from the pen of Frost's own biographer. And yet both the adulation and resentment had one thing in common: a nearly total misconception of what Frost was all about.

He is generally regarded as the poet of the countryside, of rural settings—as a folksy, crusty, wisecracking old gentleman farmer, generally of positive disposition. In short, as American as apple pie. To be fair, he greatly enhanced this notion by projecting precisely this image of himself in numerous public appearances and interviews throughout his career. I suppose it wasn't that difficult for him to do, for he had those qualities in him as well. He was indeed a quintessential American poet; it is up to us, however, to find out what that quintessence is made of, and what the term "American" means as applied to poetry and, perhaps, in general.

In 1959, at a banquet thrown in New York on the occasion of Robert Frost's eighty-fifth birthday, the most prominent literary critic at that time, Lionel Trilling, rose and, goblet in hand, declared that Robert Frost was "a terrifying poet." That, of course, caused a certain stir, but the epithet was well chosen.

Now, I want you to make the distinction here between terrifying and tragic. Tragedy, as you know, is always a *fait accompli*, whereas terror always has to do with anticipation, with man's recognition of his own negative potential—with his sense of what he is capable of. And it is the latter that was Frost's forte, not the former. In other words, his posture is radically different from the Continental tradition of the poet as tragic hero. And that difference alone makes him—for want of a better term —American.

On the surface, he looks very positively predisposed toward his surroundings—particularly toward nature. His fluency, indeed, his "being versed in country things" alone can produce this impression. However, there is a difference between the way a European perceives nature and the way an American does. Addressing this difference, W. H. Auden, in his short essay on Frost (perhaps the best thing on the poet), suggests something to the effect that when a European conceives of confronting nature, he walks out of his cottage or a little inn, filled with either friends or family, and goes for an evening stroll. If he encounters a tree, it's a tree made familiar

7

by history, to which it's been a witness. This or that king sat underneath it, laying down this or that law—something of that sort. A tree stands there rustling, as it were, with allusions. Pleased and somewhat pensive, our man, refreshed but unchanged by that encounter, returns to his inn or cottage, finds his friends or family absolutely intact, and proceeds to have a good, merry time. Whereas when an American walks out of his house and encounters a tree it is a meeting of equals. Man and tree face each other in their respective primal power, free of references: neither has a past, and as to whose future is greater, it is a toss-up. Basically, it's epidermis meeting bark. Our man returns to his cabin in a state of bewilderment, to say the least, if not in actual shock or terror.

Now, this is obviously a romantic caricature, but it accentuates the features, and that's what I am after here. In any case, the second point could be safely billed as the gist of Robert Frost's nature poetry. Nature for this poet is neither friend nor foe, nor is it the backdrop for human drama; it is this poet's terrifying self-portrait. And now I am going to start with one of his poems, which appears in the 1942 volume *A Witness Tree*. I am about to put forth my views and opinions about his lines without any concern for academic objectivity, and some of these views will be pretty dark. All I can say in my defense is (a) that I do like this poet enormously and I am going to try to sell him to you as he is, and (b) that some of that darkness is not entirely mine: it is his lines' sediment that has darkened my mind; in other words, I got it from him.

8

II

COME IN

As I came to the edge of the woods,
Thrush music—hark!
Now if it was dusk outside,
Inside it was dark.

Too dark in the woods for a bird
By sleight of wing
To better its perch for the night,
Though it still could sing.

The last of the light of the sun
That had died in the west
Still lived for one song more
In a thrush's breast.

Far in the pillared dark
Thrush music went—
Almost like a call to come in
To the dark and lament.

But no, I was out for stars:
I would not come in.
I meant not even if asked,
And I hadn't been.

Let's look at "Come In." A short poem in short meter—
actually, a combination of trimeter with dimeter, anapest
with iamb. The stuff of ballads, which by and large are
all about gore and comeuppance. So, up to a certain
point, is this poem. The meter hints as much. What are
we dealing with here? A walk in the woods? A stroll
through nature? Something that poets usually do? (And
if yes, by the way, then why?) "Come In" is one of many
poems written by Frost about such strolls. Think of "Stop-
ping by Woods on a Snowy Evening," "Acquainted with
the Night," "Desert Places," "Away!," and so forth. Or
else think of Thomas Hardy's "The Darkling Thrush,"
with which this poem has a distinct affinity. Hardy was
also very fond of lonely strolls, except most of his had a
tendency to wind up in a graveyard—since England was
settled long ago, and more thickly, I guess.

To begin with, we again have a thrush. And a bird,
as you know, is very often a bard, since, technically
speaking, both sing. So as we proceed we should bear in
mind that our poet may be delegating certain aspects of
his psyche to the bird. Actually, I firmly believe that these
two birds are related. The difference is only that it takes
Hardy sixteen lines to introduce his in a poem, whereas
Frost gets down to business in the second line. On the
whole, this is indicative of the difference between the
Americans and the British—I mean in poetry. Because
of a greater cultural heritage, a greater set of references,
it usually takes much longer for a Briton to set a poem
in motion. The sense of echo is stronger in his ear, and
thus he flexes his muscle and demonstrates his facility

before he gets down to his subject. Normally, that sort of routine results in a poem's being as big on exposition as on the actual message: in long-windedness, if you will—though, depending on who is doing the job, this is not necessarily a shortcoming.

Now, let's do it line by line. "As I came to the edge of the woods" is a fairly simple, informative job, stating the subject and setting the meter. An innocent line, on the surface, wouldn't you say? Well, it is, save for "the woods." "The woods" makes one suspicious, and, with that, "the edge" does, too. Poetry is a dame with a huge pedigree, and every word comes practically barnacled with allusions and associations. Since the fourteenth century, the woods have given off a very strong smell of *selva oscura*, and you may recall what that *selva* led the author of *The Divine Comedy* into. In any case, when a twentieth-century poet starts a poem with finding himself at the edge of the woods there is a reasonable element of danger—or, at least, a faint suggestion of it. The edge, in its very self, is sufficiently sharp.

Maybe not; maybe our suspicions are unfounded, maybe we are just paranoid and are reading too much into this line. Let's go to the next one, and we shall see:

> As I came to the edge of the woods,
> Thrush music—hark!

Looks like we've goofed. What could be more innocuous than this antiquated, Victorian-sounding, fairy-tale-like "hark"? A bird is singing—listen! "Hark" truly belongs in a Hardy poem, or in a ballad; better yet, in a jingle. It suggests a level of diction at which nothing untoward could be conveyed. The poem promises to proceed in a comforting, melodious way. That's what you're thinking, anyway, after hearing "hark": that you're going to have some sort of description of the music made by the thrush—that you are getting into familiar territory.

But that was a setup, as the following two lines show. It was but an exposition, crammed by Frost into two lines. Abruptly, in a fairly indecorous, matter-of-fact, non-melodious, and non-Victorian way, the diction and the register shift:

> Now if it was dusk outside,
> Inside it was dark.

It's "now" that does this job of leaving very little room for any fancy. What's more, you realize that the "hark" rhymes with "dark." And that that "dark" is the condition of "inside," which could allude not only to the woods, since the comma sets that "inside" into sharp opposition to the third line's "outside," and since the opposition is given you in the fourth line, which makes it a more drastic statement. Not to mention that this opposition is but the matter of substitution of just two letters: of putting *ar* instead of *us* between *d* and *k*. The vowel sound remains essentially the same. What we've got here is the difference in just one consonant.

There is a slight choking air in the fourth line. That has to do with its distribution of stresses, different from the first dimeter. The stanza contracts, as it were, toward its end, and the caesura after "inside" only underscores that "inside" 's isolation. Now, while I am offering you this deliberately slanted reading of this poem, I'd like to urge you to pay very close attention to its every letter, every cacsura, if only because it deals with a bird, and a bird's trills are a matter of pauses and, if you will, characters. Being predominantly monosyllabic, English is highly suitable for this parroting job, and the shorter the meter, the greater the pressure upon every letter, every caesura, every comma. At any rate, that "dark" literally renders the "woods" as *la selva oscura*.

With the memory of what that dark wood was entry to, let's approach the next stanza:

> Too dark in the woods for a bird
> By sleight of wing
> To better its perch for the night,
> Though it still could sing.

What do you think is happening here? A British or a Continental—or, for that matter, a properly American—innocent would still reply that it is about a bird singing in the evening, and that it is a nice tune. Interestingly, he would be right, and it is on this sort of rightness that Frost's reputation rests. In fact, though, this stanza, in particular, is extremely dark. One could argue that the poem considers something rather unpleasant, quite possibly a suicide. Or, if not suicide—well, death.

And, if not necessarily death, then—at least, in this stanza—the notion of the afterlife.

In "Too dark in the woods for a bird," a bird, alias bard, scrutinizes "the woods" and finds them too dark. "Too" here echoes—no! harks back to—Dante's opening lines in *The Divine Comedy*: our bird/bard's assessment of that *selva* differs from the great Italian's. To put it plainly, the afterlife is darker for Frost than it is for Dante. The question is why, and the answer is either because he disbelieves in the whole thing or because his notion of himself makes him, in his mind, slated for damnation. Nothing in his power can improve his eventual standing, and I'd venture that "sleight of wing" could be regarded as a reference to last rites. Above all, this poem is about being old and pondering what is next. "To better its perch for the night" has to do with the possibility of being assigned elsewhere, not just to hell—the night here being that of eternity. The only thing the bird/bard has to show for himself is that it/he "still could sing."

"The woods" are "too dark" for a bird because a bird is too far gone at being a bird. No motion of its soul, alias "sleight of wing," can improve its eventual fate in these "woods." Whose woods these are I think we know: one of their branches is where a bird is to end up anyway, and a "perch" gives a sense of these woods' being well structured: it is an enclosure—a sort of chicken coop, if you will. Thus, our bird is doomed; no last-minute conversion ("sleight" is a conjuring term) is feasible, if only because a bard is too old for any quick motion of the hand. Yet, old though he is, he still can sing.

And in the third stanza you have that bird singing: you have the song itself, the last one. It is a tremendously expansive gesture. Look at how every word here postpones the next one. "The last"—caesura—"of the light"— caesura—"of the sun"—line break, which is a big caesura—"That had died"—caesura—"in the west." Our bird/bard traces the last of the light to its vanished source. You almost hear in this line the good old "Shenandoah," the song of going West. Delay and postponement are palpable here. "The last" is not finite, and "of the light" is not finite, and "of the sun" is not. What's more, "that had died" itself is not finite, though it should have been. Even "in the west" isn't. What we've got here is the song of lingering: of light, of life. You almost see the finger pointing out the source and then, in the broad circular motion of the last two lines, returning to the speaker in "Still lived"—caesura—"for one song more"—line break—"In a thrush's breast." Between "The last" and "breast" our poet covers an extraordinary distance: the width of the continent, if you will. After all, he describes the light, which is still upon him, the opposite of the darkness of the woods. The breast is, after all, the source of any song, and you almost see here not so much a thrush as a robin; anyhow, a bird singing at sunset: it lingers on the bird's breast.

And here, in the opening lines of the fourth stanza, is where the bird and the bard part ways. "Far in the pillared dark / Thrush music went—." The key word here is "pillared," of course: it suggests a cathedral interior—a church, in any case. In other words, our thrush flies into the woods, and you hear his music from within, "almost like a call to come in / To the dark and lament." If you want, you may replace "lament" with "repent": the effect will be practically the same. What's being described here is one of the choices before our old bard this evening: the choice he does not make. The thrush has chosen that "sleight of wing" after all. It is bettering its perch for the night; it accepts its fate, for lament is acceptance. You could plunge yourself here into a maze of ecclesiastical distinctions—Frost's essential Protestantism, etc. I'd advise against it, since a stoic posture befits believers and agnostics alike; in this line of work, it is practically inescapable. On the whole, references (religious ones especially) are not to be shrunk to inferences.

"But no, I was out for stars" is Frost's usual deceptive maneuver, projecting his positive sensibility: lines like that are what earned him his reputation. If he was indeed "out for stars," why didn't he mention that before? Why did he write the whole poem about something else? But this line is here not solely to deceive you. It is here to deceive—or, rather, to quell—himself. This whole stanza is. Unless we read this line as the poet's general statement about his presence in this world—in the romantic key, that is, as a line about his general metaphysical appetite, not to be quenched by this little one-night agony.

> I would not come in.
> I meant not even if asked,
> And I hadn't been.

There is too much jocular vehemence in these lines for us to take them at face value, although we should not omit this option, either. The man is shielding himself from his own insights, and he gets grammatically as well as syllabically assertive and less idiomatic—especially in the second line, "I would not come in," which could be easily truncated into "I *won't* come in." "I meant not even if asked" comes off with a menacing resoluteness, which could amount to a statement of his agnosticism were it not for the last line's all too clever qualifier: "And I hadn't been." This is indeed a sleight of hand.

Or else you can treat this stanza and, with it, the whole poem as Frost's humble footnote or postscript to Dante's *Commedia*, which ends with "stars"—as his acknowledgment of possessing either a lesser belief or a lesser gift. The poet here refuses an invitation into darkness; moreover, he questions the very call: "*Almost* like a call to come in . . ." One shouldn't make heavy weather of Frost's affinity with Dante, but here and there it's palpable, especially in the poems dealing with dark nights of the soul—for instance, in "Acquainted with the Night." Unlike a number of his illustrious contemporaries, Frost never wears his learning on his sleeve—mainly because it is in his bloodstream. So "I meant not even if asked" could be read not only as his refusal to make a meal of his dreadful apprehension but also as a reference to his stylistic choice in ruling out a major form. Be that as it may, one thing is clear: without Dante's *Commedia*, this poem wouldn't have existed.

Still, should you choose to read "Come In" as a nature poem, you are perfectly welcome to it. I suggest, though, that you take a longer look at the title. The twenty lines of the poem constitute, as it were, the title's translation. And in this translation, I am afraid, the expression "come in" means "die."

I I I

While in "Come In" we have Frost at his lyrical best, in "Home Burial" we have him at his narrative best. Actually, "Home Burial" is not a narrative; it is an eclogue. Or, more exactly, it is a pastoral—except that it is a very dark one. Insofar as it tells a story, it is, of course, a narrative; the means of that story's transportation, though, is dialogue, and it is the means of transportation that defines a genre. Invented by Theocritus in his idylls, refined by Virgil in the poems he called eclogues or bucolics, the pastoral is essentially an exchange between two or more characters in a rural setting, returning often to that perennial subject, love. Since the English and French word "pastoral" is overburdened with happy connotations, and since Frost is closer to Virgil than to Theocritus, and not only chronologically, let's follow Virgil and call this poem an eclogue. The rural setting is here, and so are the two characters: a farmer and his wife, who may qualify as a shepherd and a shepherdess, except that it is two thousand years later. So is their subject: love, two thousand years later.

To make a long story short, Frost is a very Virgilian poet. By that, I mean the Virgil of the *Bucolics* and the *Georgics*, not the Virgil of the *Aeneid*. To begin with, the young Frost did a considerable amount of farming— as well as a lot of writing. The posture of gentleman farmer wasn't all posture. As a matter of fact, until the end of his days he kept buying farms. By the time he died, he had owned, if I am not mistaken, four farms in Vermont and New Hampshire. He knew something about living off the land—not less, in any case, than Virgil, who must have been a disastrous farmer, to judge by the agricultural advice he dispenses in the *Georgics*.

With few exceptions, American poetry is essentially Virgilian, which is to say contemplative. That is, if you take four Roman poets of the Augustan period, Propertius, Ovid, Virgil, and Horace, as the standard representatives of the four known humors (Propertius' choleric intensity, Ovid's sanguine couplings, Virgil's phlegmatic musings, Horace's melancholic equipoise), then American poetry—indeed, poetry in English in general— strikes you as being by and large of Virgilian or Horatian denomination. (Consider the bulk of Wallace Stevens's soliloquies, or the late, American Auden.) Yet Frost's affinity with Virgil is not so much temperamental as technical. Apart from frequent recourse to disguise (or mask) and the opportunity for distancing oneself that an invented character offers to the poet, Frost and Virgil have in common a tendency to hide the real subject matter of their dialogues under the monotonous, opaque sheen of their respective pentameters and hexameters. A poet of extraordinary probing and anxiety, the Virgil of the *Eclogues* and the *Georgics* is commonly taken for a bard of love and country pleasures, just like the author of *North of Boston*.

To this it should be added that Virgil in Frost comes to you obscured by Wordsworth and Browning. "Filtered" is perhaps a better word, and Browning's dramatic monologue is quite a filter, engulfing the dramatic situation in solid Victorian ambivalence and uncertainty. Frost's dark pastorals are dramatic also, not only in the sense of the intensity of the characters' interplay but above all in the sense that they are indeed theatrical. It is a kind of theater in which the author plays all the roles, including those of stage designer, director, ballet master, etc. It's he who turns the lights off, and sometimes he is the audience also.

That stands to reason. For Theocritus' idylls, like nearly all Augustan poetry, in their own right are but a compression of Greek drama. In "Home Burial" we have an arena reduced to a staircase, with its Hitchcockian banister. The opening line tells you as much about the actors' positions as about their roles: those of the hunter and his prey. Or, as you'll see later, of Pygmalion and Galatea, except that in this case the sculptor turns his living model into stone. In the final analysis, "Home Burial" is a love poem, and if only on these grounds it qualifies as a pastoral.

But let's examine this line and a half:

He saw her from the bottom of the stairs
Before she saw him.

Frost could have stopped right here. It is already a
poem, it is already a drama. Imagine this line and a half
sitting on the page all by itself, in minimalist fashion.
It's an extremely loaded scene—or, better yet, a frame.
You've got an enclosure, the house, with two individuals
at cross—no, diverse—purposes. He's at the bottom of
the stairs; she's at the top. He's looking up at her; she,
for all we know thus far, doesn't register his presence at
all. Also, you've got to remember that it's in black and
white. The staircase dividing them suggests a hierarchy
of significances. It is a pedestal with her atop (at least, in
his eyes) and him at the bottom (in our eyes and, even-
tually, in hers). The angle is sharp. Place yourself here
in either position—better in his—and you'll see what I
mean. Imagine yourself observing, watching somebody,
or imagine yourself being watched. Imagine yourself in-
terpreting someone's movements—or immobility—un-
beknownst to that person. That's what turns you into a
hunter, or into Pygmalion.

Let me press this Pygmalion business a bit further.
Scrutiny and interpretation are the gist of any intense
human interplay, and of love in particular. They are also
the most powerful source of literature: of fiction (which
is by and large about betrayal) and, above all, of lyric
poetry, where one is trying to figure out the beloved and
what makes her/him tick. And this figuring out brings us
back to the Pygmalion business quite literally, since the

more you chisel out and the more you penetrate the character, the more you put your model on a pedestal. An enclosure—be it a house, a studio, a page—intensifies this pedestal aspect enormously. And, depending on your industry and on the model's ability to cooperate, this process results either in a masterpiece or in a disaster. In "Home Burial" it results in both. For every Galatea is ultimately a Pygmalion's self-projection. On the other hand, art doesn't imitate life but infects it.

So let's watch the deportment of the model:

> She was starting down,
> Looking back over her shoulder at some fear.
> She took a doubtful step and then undid it
> To raise herself and look again.

On the literal level, on the level of straight narrative, we have the heroine beginning to descend the steps with her head turned to us in profile, her glance lingering on some frightful sight. She hesitates and interrupts her descent, her eyes still trained, presumably, on the same sight: neither on the steps nor on the man at the bottom. But you are aware of yet another level present here, aren't you?

Let's leave that level as yet unnamed. Each piece of information in this narrative comes to you in an isolated manner, within a pentameter line. The isolation job is done by white margins framing, as it were, the whole scene, like the silence of the house; and the lines themselves are the staircase. Basically, what you get here is a succession of frames. "She was starting down" is one frame. "Looking back over her shoulder at some fear" is another; in fact, it is a close-up, a profile—you see her facial expression. "She took a doubtful step and then undid it" is a third: again a close-up—the feet. "To raise herself and look again" is a fourth—full figure.

But this is a ballet, too. There is a minimum of two *pas de deux* here, conveyed to you with a wonderful euphonic, almost alliterative precision. I mean the *d*s in this line, in "doubtful" and in "undid it," although the *t*s matter also. "Undid it" is particularly good, because you sense the spring in that step. And that profile in its opposition to the movement of the body—the very formula of a dramatic heroine—is straight out of a ballet as well.

But the real *faux pas de deux* starts with "He spoke / Advancing toward her." For the next twenty-five lines, a conversation occurs on the stairs. The man climbs them as he speaks, negotiating mechanically and verbally what separates them. "Advancing" bespeaks self-consciousness and apprehensiveness. The tension grows with the growing proximity. However, the mechanical and, by implication, physical proximity is more easily attained than the verbal—i.e., the mental—and that's what the poem is all about. " 'What is it you see / From up there always?—for I want to know' " is very much a Pygmalion question, addressed to the model on the pedestal: atop the staircase. His fascination is not with what he sees but with what he imagines it conceals—what he has placed there. He invests her with mystery and then rushes to uncloak it: this rapacity is always Pygmalion's double bind. It is as though the sculptor found himself puzzled by the facial expression of his model: she "sees" what he does not "see." So he has to climb to the pedestal himself, to put himself in her position. In the position of "up there always"—of topographical (vis-à-vis the house) and psychological advantage, where he put her himself. It is the latter, the psychological advantage of the creation, that disturbs the creator, as the emphatic " 'for I want to know' " shows.

The model refuses to cooperate. In the next frame ("She turned and sank upon her skirts at that"), followed by the close-up of "And her face changed from terrified to dull," you get that lack of cooperation plain. Yet the lack of cooperation here *is* cooperation. The less you cooperate, the more you are a Galatea. For we have to bear in mind that the woman's psychological advantage is in the man's self-projection. He ascribes it to her. So by turning him down she only enhances his fantasy. In this sense, by refusing to cooperate she plays along. That's basically her whole game here. The more he climbs, the greater is that advantage; he pushes her into it, as it were, with every step.

Still, he is climbing: in "he said to gain time" he does, and also in

> "What is it you see?"
> Mounting until she cowered under him.
> "I will find out now—you must tell me, dear."

The most important word here is the verb "see," which we encounter for the second time. In the next nine lines, it will be used four more times. We'll get to that in a minute. But first let's deal with this "mounting" line and the next. It's a masterly job here. With "mounting," the poet kills two birds at once, for "mounting" describes both the climb and the climber. And the climber looms even larger, because the woman "cowers"—i.e., shrinks under him. Remember that she looks "at some fear." "Mounting" versus "cowered" gives you the contrast, then, between their respective frames, with the implicit danger contained in his largeness. In any case, her alternative to fear is not comfort. And the resoluteness of " 'I will find out now' " echoes the superior physical mass, not alleviated by the cajoling "dear" that follows a remark—" 'you must tell me' " that is both imperative and conscious of this contrast.

> She, in her place, refused him any help,
> With the least stiffening of her neck and silence.
> She let him look, sure that he wouldn't see,
> Blind creature; and awhile he didn't see
> But at last he murmured, "Oh," and again, "Oh."
>
> "What is it—what?" she said.
>
> "Just that I see."
>
> "You don't," she challenged. "Tell me what it is."
>
> "The wonder is I didn't see at once."

And now we come to this verb "see." Within fifteen lines it's been used six times. Every experienced poet knows how risky it is to use the same word several times within a short space. The risk is that of tautology. So what is it that Frost is after here? I think he is after precisely that: tautology. More accurately, nonsemantic utterance. Which you get, for instance, in " 'Oh,' and again, 'Oh.' " Frost had a theory about what he called "sentence-sounds." It had to do with his observation that the sound, the tonality, of human locution is as semantic as actual words. For instance, you overhear two people conversing behind a closed door, in a room. You don't hear the words, yet you know the general drift of their dialogue; in fact, you may pretty accurately figure out its substance. In other words, the tune matters more than the lyrics, which are, so to speak, replaceable or redundant. Anyway, the repetition of this or that word liberates the tune, makes it more audible. By the same token, such repetition liberates the mind—rids you of the notion presented by the word. (This is the old Zen technique, of course, but, come to think of it, finding it in an American poem makes you wonder whether philosophical principles don't spring from texts rather than the other way around.)

The six "see"s here do precisely that. They exclaim rather than explain. It could be "see," it could be "Oh," it could be "yes," it could be any monosyllabic word. The idea is to explode the verb from within, for the content of the actual observation defeats the process of observation, its means, and the very observer. The effect that Frost tries to create is the inadequacy of response when you automatically repeat the first word that comes to your tongue. "Seeing" here is simply reeling from the unnameable. The least seeing our hero does is in " 'Just that I see,' " for by this time the verb, having already been used four times, is robbed of its "observing" and "understanding" meaning (not to mention the fact—draining the word even further of content—that we readers are ourselves still in the dark, still don't know what there is to see out that window). By now, it is just sound, denoting an animal response rather than a rational one.

This sort of explosion of bona-fide words into pure, nonsemantic sounds will occur several times in the course of this poem. Another happens very soon, ten lines later. Characteristically, these explosions occur whenever the players find themselves in close physical proximity. They are the verbal—or, better yet, the audial—equivalents of a hiatus. Frost directs them with tremendous consistency, suggesting his characters' profound (at least, prior to this scene) incompatibility. "Home Burial" is, in fact, the study of that, and on the literal level the tragedy it describes is the characters' comeuppance for violating each other's territorial and mental imperatives by having a child. Now that the child is lost, the imperatives play themselves out with vehemence: they claim their own.

27

I V

By standing next to the woman, the man acquires her vantage point. Because he is larger than she, and also because this is *his* house (as line 23 shows), where he has lived, presumably, most of his life, he must, one imagines, bend somewhat to put his eyes on her line of vision. Now they are next to each other, in an almost intimate proximity, on the threshold of their bedroom, atop the stairs. The bedroom has a window; a window has a view. And here Frost produces the most stunning simile of this poem, and perhaps of his entire career:

> "The wonder is I didn't see at once.
> I never noticed it from here before.
> I must be wonted to it—that's the reason.
> The little graveyard where my people are!
> So small the window frames the whole of it.
> Not so much larger than a bedroom, is it?
> There are three stones of slate and one of marble,
> Broad-shouldered little slabs there in the sunlight
> On the sidehill. We haven't to mind *those*.
> But I understand: it is not the stones,
> But the child's mound—"

" 'The little graveyard where my people are!' " generates an air of endearment, and it's with this air that " 'So small the window frames the whole of it' " starts, only to tumble itself into " 'Not so much larger than a bedroom, is it?' " The key word here is "frames," because it doubles as the window's actual frame and as a picture on a bedroom wall. The window hangs, as it were, on the bedroom wall like a picture, and that picture depicts a graveyard. "Depicting," though, means reducing to the size of a picture. Imagine having that in your bedroom. In the next line, though, the graveyard is restored to its actual size and, for that reason, equated with the bedroom. This equation is as much psychological as it is spatial. Inadvertently, the man blurts out the summary of the marriage (foreshadowed in the grim pun of the title). And, equally inadvertently, the "is it?" invites the woman to agree with this summary, almost implying her complicity.

As if that were not enough, the next two lines, with their stones of slate and marble, proceed to reinforce the simile, equating the graveyard with the made-up bed, with its pentametrically arranged pillows and cushions—populated by a family of small, inanimate children: "Broad-shouldered little slabs." This is Pygmalion unbound, on a rampage. What we have here is the man's intrusion into the woman's mind, a violation of her mental imperative—if you will, an ossification of it. And then this ossifying hand—petrifying, actually—stretches toward what's still raw, palpably as well as in her mind:

> "But I understand: it is not the stones,
> But the child's mound—"

It's not that the contrast between the stones and the mound is too stark, though it is; it is his ability—or, rather, his attempt—to articulate it that she finds unbearable. For, should he succeed, should he find the words to articulate her mental anguish, the mound will join the stones in the "picture," will become a slab itself, will become a pillow of their bed. Moreover, this will amount to the total penetration of her inner sanctum: that of her mind. And he is getting there:

> "Don't, don't, don't,
> don't," she cried.

> She withdrew, shrinking from beneath his arm
> That rested on the banister, and slid downstairs;
> And turned on him with such a daunting look,
> He said twice over before he knew himself:
> "Can't a man speak of his own child he's lost?"

The poem is gathering its dark force. Four "don't"s are that nonsemantic explosion, resulting in hiatus. We are so much in the story line now—up to the eyebrows —that we may forget that this is still a ballet, still a succession of frames, still an artifice, stage-managed by the poet. In fact, we are about to take sides with our characters, aren't we? Well, I suggest we pull ourselves out of this by our eyebrows and think for a moment about what it all tells us about our poet. Imagine, for instance, that the story line has been drawn from experience— from, say, the loss of a firstborn. What does all that you've read thus far tell you about the author, about his sensibility? How much he is absorbed by the story and—what's more crucial—to what degree he is free from it?

Were this a seminar, I'd wait for your answers. Since it is not, I've got to answer this question myself. And the answer is: He is very free. Dangerously so. The very ability to utilize—to play with—this sort of material suggests an extremely wide margin of detachment. The ability to turn this material into a blank-verse, pentameter monotone adds another degree to that detachment. To observe a relation between a family graveyard and a bedroom's four-poster—still another. Added up, they amount to a considerable degree of detachment. A degree that dooms human interplay, that makes communication impossible, for communication requires an equal. This is very much the predicament of Pygmalion vis-à-vis his model. So it's not that the story the poem tells is autobiographical but that the poem is the author's self-portrait. That is why one abhors literary biography because it is reductive. That is why I am resisting issuing you with actual data on Frost.

Where does he go, you may ask, with all that detachment? The answer is: into utter autonomy. It is from there that he observes similarities among unlike things, it is from there that he imitates the vernacular. Would you like to meet Mr. Frost? Then read his poems, nothing else; otherwise, you are in for criticism from below. Would you like to be him? Would you like to become Robert Frost? Perhaps one should be advised against such aspirations. For a sensibility like this, there is very little hope of real human congeniality, or conjugality either;

and, actually, there is very little romantic dirt on him—
of the sort normally indicative of such hope.

This is not necessarily a digression, but let's get back
to the lines. Remember the hiatus, and what causes it,
and remember that this is an artifice. Actually, the author
himself reminds you of it with

> She withdrew, shrinking from beneath his arm
> That rested on the banister, and slid downstairs . . .

It is still a ballet, you see, and the stage direction is
incorporated into the text. The most telling detail here
is the banister. Why does the author put it here? First,
to reintroduce the staircase, which we might by now have
forgotten about, stunned by the business of ruining the
bedroom. But, secondly, the banister prefigures her slid-
ing downstairs, since every child uses banisters for sliding
down. "And turned on him with such a daunting look"
is another stage direction.

> He said twice over before he knew himself:
> "Can't a man speak of his own child he's lost?"

Now, this is a remarkably good line. It has a dis-
tinctly vernacular, almost proverbial air. And the author
is definitely aware of how good it is. So, trying both to
underscore its effectiveness and to obscure his awareness
of it, he emphasizes the unwittingness of this utterance:
"He said twice over before he knew himself." On the
literal, narrative level, we have the man stunned by the

woman's gaze, the daunting look, and groping for words. Frost was awfully good with those formulaic, quasi-proverbial one-liners. "For to be social is to be forgiving" (in "The Star-Splitter"), or "The best way out is always through" ("A Servant to Servants"), for example. And a few lines later you are going to get yet another one. They are mostly pentametric; iambic pentameter is very congenial to that sort of job.

This whole section of the poem, from " 'Don't, don't, don't, don't' " on, obviously has some sexual connotations, of her turning the man down. That's what the story of Pygmalion and his model is all about. On the literal level, "Home Burial" evolves along similar "hard to get" lines. However, I don't think that Frost, for all his autonomy, was conscious of that. (After all, *North of Boston* shows no acquaintance with Freudian terminology.) And, if he was not, this sort of approach on our part is invalid. Nevertheless, we should bear some of it in mind as we are embarking on the bulk of this poem:

"Not you! —Oh, where's my hat? Oh, I don't need it!
I must get out of here. I must get air.—
I don't know rightly whether any man can."

"Amy! Don't go to someone else this time.
Listen to me. I won't come down the stairs."
He sat and fixed his chin between his fists.
"There's something I should like to ask you, dear."

"You don't know how to ask it."

"Help me, then."

Her fingers moved the latch for all reply.

V

What we've got here is the desire to escape: not so much the man as the enclosure of the place, not to mention the subject of their exchange. Yet the resolution is incomplete, as the fidgeting with the hat shows, since the execution of this desire will be counterproductive for the model as far as being the subject of explication goes. May I go so far as to suggest that that would mean a loss of advantage, not to mention that it would be the end of the poem? In fact, it does end with precisely that, with her exit. The literal level will get into conflict, or fusion, with the metaphorical. Hence " 'I don't know rightly whether any man can,' " which fuses both these levels, forcing the poem to proceed; you don't know any longer who is the horse here, who is the cart. I doubt whether the poet himself knew that at this point. The fusion's result is the release of a certain force, which subordinates his pen, and the best it can do is keep both strands— literal and metaphorical—in check.

We learn the heroine's name, and that this sort of discourse had its precedents, with nearly identical results. Given the fact that we know the way the poem ends, we may judge—well, we may imagine—the character of those occasions. The scene in "Home Burial" is but a

repetition. By this token, the poem doesn't so much in-
form us about their life as replace it. We also learn, from
" 'Don't go to someone else this time,' " about a mixture
of jealousy and sense of shame felt by at least one of
them. And we learn, from " 'I won't come down the
stairs' " and from "He sat and fixed his chin between his
fists," about the fear of violence present in their physical
proximity. The latter line is a wonderful embodiment of
stasis, very much in the fashion of Rodin's *Penseur*, albeit
with two fists, which is a very telling self-referential detail,
since the forceful application of fist to chin is what results
in a knockout.

The main thing here, though, is the reintroduction
of the stairs. Not only the literal stairs but the steps in
"he sat," too. From now on, the entire dialogue occurs
on the stairs, though they have become the scene of an
impasse rather than a passage. No physical steps are taken.
Instead, we have their verbal, or oral, substitute. The
ballet ends, yielding to the verbal advance and retreat,
which is heralded by " 'There's something I should like
to ask you, dear.' " Note again the air of cajoling, colored
this time with the recognition of its futility in "dear."
Note also the last semblance of actual interplay in " 'You
don't know how to ask it.' 'Help me, then' "—this last
knocking on the door, or, better yet, on the wall. Note
"Her fingers moved the latch for all reply," because this
feint of trying for the door is the last physical movement,
the last theatrical or cinematic gesture in the poem, save
one more latch-trying.

"My words are nearly always an offense.
I don't know how to speak of anything
So as to please you. But I might be taught,
I should suppose. I can't say I see how.
A man must partly give up being a man
With womenfolk. We could have some arrangement
By which I'd bind myself to keep hands off
Anything special you're a-mind to name.
Though I don't like such things 'twixt those that love.
Two that don't love can't live together without them.
But two that do can't live together with them."
She moved the latch a little.

The speaker's hectic mental pacing is fully counterbalanced by his immobility. If this is a ballet, it is a mental one. In fact, it's very much like fencing: not with an opponent or a shadow but with one's self. The lines are constantly taking a step forward and then undoing it. ("She took a doubtful step and then undid it.") The main technical device here is enjambment, which physically resembles descending the stairs. In fact, this back-and-forth, this give-and-take almost gives you a sense of being short of breath. Until, that is, the release that is coming with the formulaic, folksy " 'A man must partly give up being a man / With womenfolk.' "

After this release, you get three lines of more evenly paced verse, almost a tribute to iambic pentameter's proclivity for coherence, ending with the pentametrically triumphant " 'Though I don't like such things 'twixt those

that love.' " And here our poet makes another not so
subdued dash toward the proverbial: " 'Two that don't
love can't live together without them. / But two that do
can't live together with them' "—though this comes off
as a bit cumbersome, and not entirely convincing.

Frost partly senses that: hence "She moved the latch
a little." But that's only one explanation. The whole point
of this qualifier-burdened monologue is the explication
of its addressee. The man is groping for understanding.
He realizes that in order to understand he's got to sur-
render—if not suspend entirely—his rationality. In other
words, he descends. But this is really running down stairs
that lead upward. And, partly from rapidly approaching
the end of his wits, partly out of purely rhetorical inertia,
he summons here the notion of love. In other words, this
quasi-proverbial two liner about love is a rational argu-
ment, and that, of course, is not enough for its addressee.

For the more she is explicated, the more remote she
gets: the higher her pedestal grows (which is perhaps of
specific importance to her now that she is downstairs).
It's not grief that drives her out of the house but the dread
of being explicated, as well as of the explicator himself.
She wants to stay impenetrable and won't accept anything
short of his complete surrender. And he is well on the
way to it:

> "Don't—don't go.
> Don't carry it to someone else this time.
> Tell me about it if it's something human."

The last is the most stunning, most tragic line, in my view, in the entire poem. It amounts practically to the heroine's ultimate victory—i.e., to the aforementioned rational surrender on the part of the explicator. For all its colloquial air, it promotes her mental operations to supernatural status, thus acknowledging infinity —ushered into her mind by the child's death—as his rival. Against this he is powerless, since her access to that infinity, her absorption by and commerce with it, is backed in his eyes by the whole mythology of the opposite sex—by the whole notion of the alternative being impressed upon him by her at this point rather thoroughly. That's what he is losing her to by staying rational. It is a shrill, almost hysterical line, admitting the man's limitations and momentarily bringing the whole discourse to a plane of regard that the heroine could be at home on —the one she perhaps seeks. But only momentarily. He can't proceed at this level, and succumbs to pleading:

> "Let me into your grief. I'm not so much
> Unlike other folks as your standing there
> Apart would make me out. Give me my chance.
> I do think, though, you overdo it a little.
> What was it brought you up to think it the thing
> To take your mother-loss of a first child
> So inconsolably—in the face of love.
> You'd think his memory might be satisfied—"

He tumbles down, as it were, from the hysterical height of " 'Tell me about it if it's something human.' "

But this tumble, this mental knocking about the metrically lapsing stairs, restores him to rationality, with all its attendant qualifiers. That brings him rather close to the heart of the matter—to her taking her " 'mother-loss of a first child / So inconsolably' "—and he evokes the catchall notion of love again, this time somewhat more convincingly, though still tinged with a rhetorical flourish: " 'in the face of love.' " The very word—"love"— undermines its emotional reality, reducing the sentiment to its utilitarian application: as a means of overcoming tragedy. However, overcoming tragedy deprives its victim of the status of hero or heroine. This, combined with the resentment over the explicator's lowering of his explication's plane of regard, results in the heroine's interruption of " 'You'd think his memory might be satisfied—' " with " 'There you go sneering now!' " It's Galatea's self-defense, the defense against the further application of the chiseling instrument to her already attained features.

Because of its absorbing story line, there is a strong temptation to bill "Home Burial" as a tragedy of incommunicability, a poem about the failure of language; and many have succumbed to this temptation. In fact, it is just the reverse: it is a tragedy of communication, for communication's logical end is the violation of your interlocutor's mental imperative. This is a poem about language's terrifying success, for language, in the final analysis, is alien to the sentiments it articulates. No one is more aware of that than a poet; and if "Home Burial" is autobiographical, it is so in the first place by revealing Frost's grasp of the collision between his métier and his emotions. To drive this point home, may I suggest that you compare the actual sentiment you may feel toward an individual in your company and the word "love." A poet is doomed to resort to words. So is the speaker in "Home Burial." Hence, their overlapping in this poem; hence, too, its autobiographical reputation.

But let us take it a step further. The poet here should be identified not with one character but with both. He is the man here, all right, but he is the woman also. Thus you've got a clash not just of two sensibilities but of two languages. Sensibilities may merge—say, in the act of love; languages can't. Sensibilities may result in a child; languages won't. And, now that the child is dead, what's left is two totally autonomous languages, two non-overlapping systems of verbalization. In short: words. His versus hers, and hers are fewer. This makes her enigmatic. Enigmas are subject to explication, which they resist— in her case, with all she's got. His job, or, more exactly, the job of his language, is, therefore, the explication of her language, or, more exactly, her reticence. Which, when it comes to human interplay, is a recipe for disaster. When it comes to a poem, an enormous challenge.

Small wonder, then, that this "dark pastoral" grows darker with every line; it proceeds by aggravation, reflecting not so much the complexity of the author's mind as words' own appetite for disaster. For the more you push reticence, the greater it gets, having nothing to fall back upon but itself. The enigma thus grows bigger. It's like Napoleon invading Russia and finding that it goes beyond the Urals. Small wonder that this "dark pastoral" of ours has no choice but to proceed by aggravation, for the poet's mind plays both the invading army and the territory; in the end, he can't take sides. It is a sense of the incomprehensible vastness of what lies ahead, defeating not only the notion of conquest but the very sense of progress, that informs both " 'Tell me about it if it's something human' " and the lines that follow " 'There you go sneering now!' ":

> "I'm not, I'm not!
> You make me angry. I'll come down to you.
> God, what a woman!"

A language invading reticence gets no trophy here, save the echo of its own words. All it has to show for its efforts is a good old line that brought it nowhere before·

> "And it's come to this,
> A man can't speak of his own child that's dead."

It, too, falls back on itself. A stalemate.

                               ·

It's broken by the woman. More exactly, her reticence is broken. Which could be regarded by the male character as success, were it not for what she surrenders. Which is not so much an offensive as a negation of all the man stands for.

"You can't because you don't know how to speak.
If you had any feelings, you that dug
With your own hand—how could you?—his little
     grave;
I saw you from that very window there,
Making the gravel leap and leap in air,
Leap up, like that, like that, and land so lightly
And roll back down the mound beside the hole.
I thought, Who is that man? I didn't know you.
And I crept down the stairs and up the stairs
To look again, and still your spade kept lifting.
Then you came in. I heard your rumbling voice
Out in the kitchen, and I don't know why,
But I went near to see with my own eyes.
You could sit there with the stains on your shoes
Of the fresh earth from your own baby's grave
And talk about your everyday concerns.
You had stood the spade up against the wall
Outside there in the entry, for I saw it."

"I shall laugh the worst laugh I ever laughed.
I'm cursed. God, if I don't believe I'm cursed."

This is the voice of a very foreign territory indeed: a foreign language. It is a view of the man from a distance he can't possibly fathom, since it is proportionate to the frequency with which the heroine creeps up and down the stairs. Which, in its own right, is proportionate to the leaps of his gravel in the course of his digging the grave. Whatever the ratio, it is not in favor of his actual or mental steps toward her on that staircase. Nor in his favor is the rationale behind her creeping up and down the stairs while he is digging. Presumably, there is nobody else around to do the job. (That they lost their firstborn suggests that they are fairly young and thus not very well off.) Presumably also, by performing this menial task, and by doing it in a particularly mechanical way—as a remarkably skillful mimetic job in the pentameter here indicates (or as is charged by the heroine)—the man is quelling, or controlling, his grief; that is, his movements, unlike the heroine's, are functional.

In short, this is futility's view of utility. For obvious reasons, this view is usually precise and rich in judgment: " 'If you had any feelings,' " and " 'Leap up, like that, like that, and land so lightly / And roll back down the mound beside the hole.' " Depending on the length of observation—and the description of digging runs here for nine lines—this view may result, as it does here, in a sensation of utter disparity between the observer and the observed: " 'I thought, Who is that man? I didn't know you.' " For observation, you see, results in nothing, while digging produces at least a mound, or a hole. Whose mental equivalent in the observer is also, as it were, a grave. Or, rather, a fusion of the man and his purpose, not to mention his instrument. What futility and Frost's pentameter register here above all is rhythm. The heroine observes an inanimate machine. The man in her eye is a gravedigger, and thus her alternative.

Now, the sight of our alternative is always unwelcome, not to say threatening. The closer your view of it, the sharper your general sense of guilt and of a deserved comeuppance. In the mind of a woman who has lost her child, that sense may be fairly sharp. Add to that her inability to translate her grief into any useful action, save a highly agitated creeping up and down, as well as the recognition—and subsequent glorification—of that inability. And add a cross-purpose correspondence between her movements and his: between her steps and his spade. What do you think it would result in? And remember that she is in *his* house, that this is the graveyard where *his* people are. And that he is a gravedigger.

> "Then you came in. I heard your rumbling voice
> Out in the kitchen, and I don't know why,
> But I went near to see with my own eyes."

Note this "and I don't know why," for here she unwittingly drifts toward her own projection. All that she needs now is to check that projection with her own eyes. That is, she wants to make her mental picture physical:

> "You could sit there with the stains on your shoes
> Of the fresh earth from your own baby's grave
> And talk about your everyday concerns.
> You had stood the spade up against the wall
> Outside there in the entry, for I saw it."

So what do you think she sees with her own eyes, and what does that sight prove? What does the frame contain this time? What does she have a close-up of? I

am afraid she sees a murder weapon: she sees a blade.
The fresh earth stains either on the shoes or on his spade
make the spade's edge shine: make it into a blade. And
does earth "stain," however fresh? Her very choice of
noun, denoting liquid, suggests—accuses—blood. What
should our man have done? Should he have taken his
shoes off before entering the house? Perhaps. Perhaps he
should have left his spade outside, too. But he is a farmer,
and acts like one—presumably out of fatigue. So he
brings in his instrument—in her eyes, the instrument of
death. And the same goes for his shoes, and it goes for
the rest of the man. A gravedigger is equated here, if you
will, with the reaper. And there are only the two of them
in this house.

The most awful bit is "for I saw it," because it em-
phasizes the perceived symbolism of that spade left stand-
ing against the wall outside there in the entry: for future
use. Or as a guard. Or as an unwilling *memento mori*.
At the same time, "for I saw it" conveys the capriciousness
of her perception and the triumph of somebody who
cannot be fooled, the triumph of catching the enemy. It
is futility in full bloom, engulfing and absorbing utility
into its shadow.

> "I shall laugh the worst laugh I ever laughed.
> I'm cursed. God, if I don't believe I'm cursed."

This is practically a nonverbal recognition of defeat, com-
ing in the form of a typical Frostian understatement,
studded with tautological monosyllables quickly aban-

doning their semantic functions. Our Napoleon or Pygmalion is completely routed by his creation, who still keeps pressing on.

> "I can repeat the very words you were saying:
> 'Three foggy mornings and one rainy day
> Will rot the best birch fence a man can build.'
> Think of it, talk like that at such a time!
> What had how long it takes a birch to rot
> To do with what was in the darkened parlor?"

Now, this is where our poem effectively ends. The rest is simply denouement, in which our heroine goes rambling on in an increasingly incoherent fashion about death, the world being evil, uncaring friends, and feeling alone. It is a rather hysterical monologue, whose only function, in terms of the story line, is to struggle toward a release for what has been pent up in her mind. It does not, and in the end she resorts to the door, as though only landscape were proportionate to her mental state and thus could be of solace.

And, quite possibly, it is. A conflict within an enclosure—a house, say—normally deteriorates into tragedy, because the rectangularity of the place itself puts a higher premium on reason, offering emotion only a straitjacket. Thus in the house the man is the master not only because the house is his but because—within the context of the poem—rationality is his. In a landscape, "Home Burial"'s dialogue would have run a different course; in a landscape, the man would be the loser. The drama would perhaps be even greater, for it's one thing when the house sides with a character, and another when the elements do so. In any case, that's why she is trying for the door.

So let's get back to the five lines that precede the denouement—to this business of rotting birches. "Three foggy mornings and one rainy day / Will rot the best birch fence a man can build," our farmer is quoted as saying, sitting there in the kitchen, clods of fresh earth on his shoes and the spade standing up there in the entry. One may ascribe this phrase again to his fatigue and to the next task in store for him: building a little fence around the new grave. However, since this is not a public but a family graveyard, the fence he mentioned might indeed be one of his everyday concerns, something else he has to deal with. And presumably he mentions it to take his mind off what he has just finished doing. Still, for all his effort, the mind is not entirely taken, as the verb "rot" indicates: the line contains the shadow of the hidden comparison—if a fence rots so quickly in the damp *air*, how quickly will a little coffin rot in earth damp enough to leave "stains" on his shoes? But the heroine once again resists the encompassing gambits of language—metaphor, irony, litotes—and goes straight for the literal meaning, the absolute. And that's what she jumps on in " 'What had how long it takes a birch to rot / To do with what was in the darkened parlor?' " What is remarkable here is how diverse their treatment of the notion of rotting is. While he is talking about a "birch fence," which is a clear deflection, not to mention a reference to something above the ground, she zeroes in on "what was in the

47

darkened parlor." It's understandable that, being a mother, she concentrates—that Frost makes her concentrate—on the dead child. Yet her way of referring to it is highly roundabout, even euphemistic: "what was in." Not to mention that she refers to her dead child as a "what," not a "who." We don't learn his name, and for all we know, he didn't have much of a life after his birth. And then you should note her reference to the grave: "the darkened parlor."

Now, with "darkened parlor," the poet finishes his portrait of the heroine. We have to bear in mind that this is a rural setting, that the heroine lives in "his" house—i.e., that she came here from without. Because of its proximity to rot, this darkened parlor, for all its colloquial currency, sounds noticeably oblique, not to say arch. To the modern ear it has an almost Victorian ring, suggesting a difference of sensibilities bordering on class distinction.

I think you will agree that this is not a European poem. Not French, not Italian, not German, not even British. I also can assure you that it is not Russian at all. And, in terms of what American poetry is like today, it is not American, either. It's Frost's own, and he has been dead for over a quarter of a century now. Small wonder, then, that one rambles on about his lines at such length, and in strange places, though he no doubt would wince at being introduced to a French audience by a Russian. On the other hand, he was no stranger to incongruity.

So what was it that he was after in this, his very own poem? He was, I think, after grief and reason, which, while poison to each other, are language's most efficient fuel—or, if you will, poetry's indelible ink. Frost's reliance on them here and elsewhere almost gives you the sense that his dipping into this ink pot had to do with the hope of reducing the level of its contents; you detect a sort of vested interest on his part. Yet the more one dips into it, the more it brims with this black essence of existence, and the more one's mind, like one's fingers, gets soiled by this liquid. For the more there is of grief, the more there is of reason. As much as one may be tempted to take sides in "Home Burial," the presence of the narrator here rules this out, for while the characters stand, respectively, for reason and for grief, the narrator stands for their fusion. To put it differently, while the characters' actual union disintegrates, the story, as it were, marries grief to reason, since the bond of the narrative here supersedes the individual dynamics—well, at least for the reader. Perhaps for the author as well. The poem, in other words, plays fate.

I suppose it is this sort of marriage that Frost was after, or perhaps the other way around. Many years ago, on a flight from New York to Detroit, I chanced upon an essay by the poet's daughter printed in the American Airlines in-flight magazine. In that essay Lesley Frost says that her father and her mother were co-valedictorians at the high school they both attended. While she doesn't recall the topic of her father's speech on that occasion, she remembers what she was told was her mother's. It was called something like "Conversation as a Force in Life" (or "the Living Force"). If, as I hope, someday you find a copy of *North of Boston* and read it, you'll realize that Elinor White's topic is, in a nutshell, the main structural device of that collection, for most of the poems in *North of Boston* are dialogues—are conversations. In this sense, we are dealing here—in "Home Burial," as elsewhere in *North of Boston*—with love poetry, or, if you will, with poetry of obsession: not that of a man with a woman so much as that of an argument with a counterargument—of a voice with a voice. That goes for monologues as well, actually, since a monologue is one's argument with oneself; take, for instance, "To be or not to be . . ." That's why poets so often resort to writing plays. In the end, of course, it was not the dialogue that Robert Frost was after but the other way around, if only because by themselves two voices amount to little. Fused, they set in motion something that, for want of a better term, we may just as well call "life." This is why "Home Burial" ends with a dash, not with a period.

HOME BURIAL

He saw her from the bottom of the stairs
Before she saw him. She was starting down,
Looking back over her shoulder at some fear.
She took a doubtful step and then undid it
To raise herself and look again. He spoke
Advancing toward her: "What is it you see
From up there always?—for I want to know."
She turned and sank upon her skirts at that,
And her face changed from terrified to dull.

He said to gain time: "What is it you see?"
Mounting until she cowered under him.
"I will find out now—you must tell me, dear."
She, in her place, refused him any help,
With the least stiffening of her neck and silence.
She let him look, sure that he wouldn't see,
Blind creature; and awhile he didn't see.
But at last he murmured, "Oh," and again, "Oh."

"What is it—what?" she said.

                        "Just that I see."

"You don't," she challenged. "Tell me what it is."

"The wonder is I didn't see at once.
I never noticed it from here before.
I must be wonted to it—that's the reason.
The little graveyard where my people are!
So small the window frames the whole of it.
Not so much larger than a bedroom, is it?
There are three stones of slate and one of marble,
Broad-shouldered little slabs there in the sunlight
On the sidehill. We haven't to mind *those*.
But I understand: it is not the stones,
But the child's mound—"

                   "Don't, don't, don't,
don't," she cried.

She withdrew, shrinking from beneath his arm
That rested on the banister, and slid downstairs;
And turned on him with such a daunting look,
He said twice over before he knew himself:
"Can't a man speak of his own child he's lost?"

"Not you!—Oh, where's my hat? Oh, I don't need it!
I must get out of here. I must get air.—
I don't know rightly whether any man can."

"Amy! Don't go to someone else this time.
Listen to me. I won't come down the stairs."
He sat and fixed his chin between his fists.
"There's something I should like to ask you, dear."

"You don't know how to ask it."

                              "Help me, then."

Her fingers moved the latch for all reply.

"My words are nearly always an offense.
I don't know how to speak of anything
So as to please you. But I might be taught,
I should suppose. I can't say I see how.
A man must partly give up being a man
With womenfolk. We could have some arrangement
By which I'd bind myself to keep hands off
Anything special you're a-mind to name.
Though I don't like such things 'twixt those that love.

Two that don't love can't live together without them.
But two that do can't live together with them."
She moved the latch a little. "Don't—don't go.
Don't carry it to someone else this time.
Tell me about it if it's something human.
Let me into your grief. I'm not so much
Unlike other folks as your standing there
Apart would make me out. Give me my chance.
I do think, though, you overdo it a little.
What was it brought you up to think it the thing
To take your mother-loss of a first child
So inconsolably—in the face of love.
You'd think his memory might be satisfied—"

"There you go sneering now!"

                              "I'm not, I'm not!
You make me angry. I'll come down to you.
God, what a woman! And it's come to this,
A man can't speak of his own child that's dead."

"You can't because you don't know how to speak.
If you had any feelings, you that dug
With your own hand—how could you?—his little
    grave;
I saw you from that very window there,
Making the gravel leap and leap in air,
Leap up, like that, like that, and land so lightly
And roll back down the mound beside the hole.
I thought, Who is that man? I didn't know you.

And I crept down the stairs and up the stairs
To look again, and still your spade kept lifting.
Then you came in. I heard your rumbling voice
Out in the kitchen, and I don't know why,
But I went near to see with my own eyes.
You could sit there with the stains on your shoes
Of the fresh earth from your own baby's grave
And talk about your everyday concerns.
You had stood the spade up against the wall
Outside there in the entry, for I saw it."

"I shall laugh the worst laugh I ever laughed.
I'm cursed. God, if I don't believe I'm cursed."

"I can repeat the very words you were saying:
'Three foggy mornings and one rainy day
Will rot the best birch fence a man can build.'
Think of it, talk like that at such a time!
What had how long it takes a birch to rot
To do with what was in the darkened parlor?
You *couldn't* care! The nearest friends can go
With anyone to death, comes so far short
They might as well not try to go at all.
No, from the time when one is sick to death,
One is alone, and he dies more alone.
Friends make pretense of following to the grave,
But before one is in it, their minds are turned
And making the best of their way back to life
And living people, and things they understand.

But the world's evil. I won't have grief so
If I can change it. Oh, I won't. I won't!"

"There, you have said it all and you feel better.
You won't go now. You're crying. Close the door.
The heart's gone out of it: why keep it up?
Amy! There's someone coming down the road!"

"You—oh, you think the talk is all. I must go—
Somewhere out of this house. How can I make
    you—"

"If—you—do!" She was opening the door wider.
"Where do you mean to go? First tell me that.
I'll follow and bring you back by force. I *will!*—"

If this poem is dark, darker still is the mind of its
maker, who plays all three roles: the man, the woman,
and the narrator. Their equal reality, taken separately or
together, is still inferior to that of the poem's author,
since "Home Burial" is but one poem among many. The
price of his autonomy is, of course, in its coloration, and
perhaps what you ultimately get out of this poem is not
its story but the vision of its ultimately autonomous
maker. The characters and the narrator are, as it were,
pushing the author out of any humanly palatable context:
he stands outside, denied re-entry, perhaps not coveting
it at all. This is the dialogue's—alias the Life Force's—
doing. And this particular posture, this utter autonomy,

strikes me as utterly American. Hence this poet's mono-
tone, his pentametric drawl: a signal from a far-distant
station. One may liken him to a spacecraft that, as the
downward pull of gravity weakens, finds itself nonetheless
in the grip of a different gravitational force: outward. The
fuel, though, is still the same: grief and reason. The only
thing that conspires against this metaphor of mine is that
American spacecraft usually return.

1994

SEAMUS HEANEY

Above the Brim

Robert Frost at his cabin on the Homer Noble Farm, Breadloaf,
Vermont, July 1948. (From the collection of Peter Stanlis)

Among major poets of the English language in this century, Robert Frost is the one who takes the most punishment. "Like a chimpanzee" is how one friend of mine remembers him in the flesh, but in the afterlife of the text he has been consigned to a far less amiable sector of the bestiary, among the stoats perhaps, or the weasels. Calculating self-publicist, reprehensible egotist, oppressive parent—theories of the death of the author have failed to lay the ghost of this vigorous old contender who beats along undauntedly at the reader's elbow. His immense popular acclaim during his own lifetime; his apotheosis into an idol mutually acceptable to his own and his country's self-esteem, and greatly inflationary of both; his constantly resourceful acclimatization of himself to this condition, as writer and performer—it all generated a critical resistance and fed a punitive strain which is never far to seek in literary circles anyhow.

Still, it would be wrong to see this poet as the unwitting victim of the fashion which he surfed upon for decades. Demonically intelligent, as acute about his own masquerades as he was about others', Frost obeyed the ancient command to know himself. Like Yeats at the end of "Dialogue of Self and Soul," Frost would be "content to live it all again," and be content also to "cast out remorse." Unlike Yeats, however, he would expect neither a flow of sweetness into his breast nor a flash of beatitude upon the world to ensue from any such bout of self-exculpation. He made no secret of the prejudice and contrariness at the center of his nature, and never shirked the bleakness of that last place in himself. He was well aware of the abrasiveness of many of his convictions and their unpopular implications in the context of New Deal politics, yet for all his archness, he did not hide those convictions or retreat from them.

Frost's appetite for his own independence was fierce and expressed itself in a reiterated belief in his right to limits: his defenses, his fences, and his freedom were all interdependent. Yet he also recognized that his compulsion to shape his own destiny and to proclaim the virtues of self-containment arose from a terror of immense, unlimited, and undefined chaos. This terror gets expressed melodramatically in a poem like "Design," and obliquely in a poem like "Provide, Provide," but it is also there in many of his more casual pronouncements. Here he is, for example, writing to Amy Bonner in June 1937:

There are no two things as important to us in life and art as being threatened and being saved. What are ideals of form for if we aren't going to be made to fear for them? All our ingenuity is lavished on getting into danger legitimately so that we may be genuinely rescued.

Frost believed, in other words, that individual venture and vision arose as a creative defense against emptiness, and that it was therefore always possible that a relapse into emptiness would be the ultimate destiny of consciousness. If good fences made good neighbors, if (as Ian Hamilton has suggested) a certain callousness of self-assertion was part of the price of adjusting to reality, Frost was ready to pay that price in terms of exclusiveness and isolation, and in terms also of guardedness and irony (and William Pritchard writes well about this in his deliberately positive study of the poet). The main thing is that Frost was prepared to look without self-deception into the crystal of indifference in himself where his moral and artistic improvisations were both prefigured and scrutinized, and in this essay I shall be concerned to show that his specifically poetic achievement is profoundly guaranteed and resilient because it is "genuinely rescued" from negative recognitions, squarely faced, and abidingly registered.

Frost was always ready to hang those negative recognitions in the balance against his more comfortable imaginings. He made it clear, for example, that there was a cold shadow figure behind the warm-blooded image of his generally beloved horseman in "Stopping by Woods on a Snowy Evening":

My little horse must think it queer
To stop without a farmhouse near
Between the woods and frozen lake
The darkest evening of the year.

He gives his harness bells a shake
To ask if there is some mistake.
The only other sound's the sweep
Of easy wind and downy flake.

This rider, faring forward against the drift of more than snow, a faithful, self-directed quester with promises to keep and miles to go before he sleeps, this figure finds his counterpart in "Desert Places," a poem of the same length, written in almost the same rhyme scheme. In "Desert Places" Frost implicitly concedes the arbitrariness of the consolations offered by the earlier poem and deliberately undermines its sureties. The social supports that were vestigially present in "promises to keep" have now been pulled away, and the domestic security of woods with owners in the village is rendered insignificant by a vacuous interstellar immensity:

Snow falling and night falling fast, oh, fast
In a field I looked into going past,
And the ground almost covered smooth in snow,
But a few weeds and stubble showing last.

The woods around it have it—it is theirs.
All animals are smothered in their lairs.

I am too absent-spirited to count;
The loneliness includes me unawares.

And lonely as it is that loneliness
Will be more lonely ere it will be less—
A blanker whiteness of benighted snow
With no expression, nothing to express.

They cannot scare me with their empty spaces
Between stars—on stars where no human race is.
I have it in me so much nearer home
To scare myself with my own desert places.

This poem gives access to the dark side of Frost, which
was always there behind the mask of Yankee hominess,
a side of him which also became fashionable late in the
day, after Lionel Trilling gave it the modernists' blessing
in a speech at Frost's eighty-fifth birthday party. Trilling
there drew attention to Frost's Sophoclean gift for making
the neuter outback of experience scrutable in a way that
privileges neither the desolate unknown nor the human
desire to shelter from it. I am going to pause with the
poem at this early stage, however, not in order to open
the vexed question of Frost's dimensions as a philosoph-
ical writer or to address the range of his themes or to
contextualize his stances, imaginative and civic, within
American political and intellectual history. All of these
things are worth considering, but I raise them only to
salute them dutifully and so pass on to my own particular
area of interest.

This arises from a lifetime of pleasure in Frost's poems as events in language, flaunts and vaunts full of projective force and deliquescent backwash, the crestings of a tide that lifts all spirits. Frost may have indeed declared that his whole anxiety was for himself as a performer, but the performance succeeded fully only when it launched itself beyond skill and ego into a run of energy that brimmed up outside the poet's conscious intention and control.

Consider, for example, the conclusion of "Desert Places," which I have just quoted: "I have it in me so much nearer home / To scare myself with my own desert places." However these lines may incline toward patness, whatever risk they run of making the speaker seem to congratulate himself too easily as an initiate of darkness, superior to the deluded common crowd, whatever trace they contain of knowingness that mars other poems by Frost, they still succeed convincingly. They overcome one's incipient misgivings and subsume them into the larger, more impersonal, and undeniable emotional occurrence which the whole poem represents.

I call it an emotional occurrence, yet it is preeminently a rhythmic one, an animation via the ear of the whole nervous apparatus: what Borges called "an almost physical emotion." The tilt of the sound is unmistakable from the beginning. The momentary stay of the stanza is being sifted away from the inside, words are running out from under themselves, and there is no guarantee that form will effect a rescue from danger:

> Snow falling and night falling fast, oh, fast
> In a field I looked into going past . . .

This meter is full of the hurry and slant of driven snow, its unstoppable, anxiety-inducing forward rush, all that whispering turmoil of a blizzard. Here the art of the language is like the art of the French farmer in "The Ax-Helve"; what is said in that poem about the lines and grains of a hickory axe shaft applies equally to the lines of "Desert Places." The French farmer

> showed me that the lines of a good helve
> Were native to the grain before the knife
> Expressed them, and its curves were no false curves
> Put on it from without.

The curves and grains of the first two lines of "Desert Places" are correspondingly native to living speech, without any tonal falsity. Who really notices that the letter *f* alliterates five times within thirteen syllables? It is no denigration of Hopkins to say that when such an alliterative cluster happens in his work, the reader is the first to notice it. With Frost, its effect is surely known, like a cold air that steals across a face; but until the lines are deliberately dwelt upon a moment like this, we do not even think of it as an "effect," and the means that produce it remain as unshowy as the grain in the wood:

> Snow falling and night falling fast, oh, fast
> In a field I looked into going past,
> And the ground almost covered smooth in snow,
> But a few weeds and stubble showing last.

This feels like an unpremeditated rush of inspiration, and Frost always declared that he liked to take a poem thus, at a single stroke, when the mood was on him. Yet even if the actual composition of "Desert Places" entailed no such speedy, pell-mell onslaught of perceptions, the finished poem does indeed induce that kind of sensation. There is an urgent, toppling pattern to it all, an urgency created by various minimal but significant verbal delicacies—like, for example, the omission of the relative pronoun from the line "In a field I looked into going past." Compare this with "In a field that I looked into going past" and hear how the inclusion of an extra syllable breaks the slippage toward panic in the line as we have it. Or consider how the end-stopping of the first eight lines does not (as we might expect) add composure to them but contributes instead a tensed-up, pent-up movement:

> The woods around it have it—it is theirs.
> All animals are smothered in their lairs.
> I am too absent-spirited to count;
> The loneliness includes me unawares.

And where does that line about being "too absent-spirited to count" arrive from? Does it mean that the

speaker does not matter? Or something else? In the on-
wardness of a reading, such curiosity registers fleetingly,
like something glimpsed from a carriage window. To
count what? The animals? The lairs? And what is "it"
that the woods have? Is it snow? Is it loneliness? The
speaker is so hypnotized by the snow swirl that he doesn't
count as consciousness anymore, he is adrift instead, in
the dream of smothered lairs. And those triple masculine
rhymes of "fast" / "past" / "last," with their monosyllabic
stress repeated again in "theirs" / "lairs" / "awares," are
like the slowing of the heartbeat in the withdrawn hi-
bernators.

Halfway through the poem, then, the narcotic aspect
of the snowfall is predominant, and the vowel music is
like a dulled pulse beat: going, covered smooth, stubble
showing, smothered. But in the next eight lines we go
through the nature barrier, as it were, into the ether of
symbolic knowledge. The consolations of being "too
absent-spirited to count" are disallowed and the poem
suddenly blinks itself out of reverie into vision. The vow-
els divest themselves of their comfortable roundness, the
rhymes go slender first and then go feminine: "loneli-
ness" / "less" / "express"; "spaces" / "race is" / "places."
The repetition which at the start was conducive to trance,
and included speaker and reader "unawares," now buzzes
everybody and everything awake.

Once again, the effect is not "put on from without,"
not a flourish of craft, but a feat of technique. There is
a disconsolateness in the way the word "lonely" keeps
rebounding off its image in the word "loneliness"; and

the same holds true for the closed-circuit energy of "expression" and "express." Finally, there is a Dantesque starkness about the repetition of the word "stars." Even if these stars are not intended to echo the *stelle* that shine at the end of each of Dante's visions, they still do possess the cold tingle of infinity. So, by such feats of mimesis and orchestration, the speaker's inwardness with all this outward blankness is established long before he declares himself explicitly in the concluding lines. And that is what I meant earlier when I spoke of the excessiveness of the language's own rightness, brimming up beyond the poet's deliberate schemes and performances:

> And lonely as it is that loneliness
> Will be more lonely ere it will be less—
> A blanker whiteness of benighted snow
> With no expression, nothing to express.

> They cannot scare me with their empty spaces
> Between stars—on stars where no human race is.
> I have it in me so much nearer home
> To scare myself with my own desert places.

Inevitably, a discussion like this, which concentrates on the poem's musical life, must lead us to take cognizance of Frost's theory of "the sound of sense." This theory, as Frost expressed it in interviews and letters over the years, does fit and complement our experience of what is distinctive about the run of his verse, its posture in the mouth and in the ear, its constant drama of tone and tune. "The sound of sense" presents itself as a technical prescription and serves notice that Frost, even though he broke with the experimental modernists, was still a poet of that critical early-twentieth-century moment, every bit as concerned as the Imagists ever were to heave the art of verse out of its backward drag into nineteenth-century musicality.

.

A few quotations will suffice to recall the basic convictions which underlay much of Frost's practice; indeed, most of them can be culled from a letter to John T. Bartlett (July 4, 1913), where he begins by distinguishing between the good and bad senses of the word "craft," the bad one applied to those poets whom he calls "mechanics." He goes on then:

To be perfectly frank with you I am one of the most notable craftsmen of my time . . . I am possibly the only person going who works on any but a worn out theory [principle I had better say] of versification . . . I alone of English writers have consciously set myself to make music out of what I may call the sound of sense. Now it is possible to have sense without the sound of sense (as in much prose that is supposed to pass muster but makes very dull reading) and the sound of sense without sense (as in Alice in Wonderland which makes anything but dull reading). The best place to get the abstract sound of sense is from voices behind a door that cuts off the words . . . It is the abstract vitality of our speech. It is pure sound—pure form. One who concerns himself with it more than the subject is

an artist . . . But if one is to be a poet he must learn to get
cadences by skillfully breaking the sounds of sense with all
their irregularity of accent across the regular beat of the metre.

This gives the main gist of Frost's poetics. It can be sup-
plemented by many other declarations about sentence-
sounds and tones of voice, all of which are designed to
give an ultimate authority to perfectly pitched natural
speech cadences realized in a written text. Such cadences,
Frost is at pains to insist, re-establish a connection with
the original springs of our human being.

Talking of sentence-sounds, for example, which he
elsewhere describes as "the most volatile and at the same
time important part of poetry" (the part we can no longer
hear in poems in ancient Greek or Latin), he maintains:

No one makes or adds to them. They are always there, living
in the cave of the mouth . . . And they are as definitely things
as any image of sight. The most creative imagination is only
their summoner.

To summon such sounds, therefore, is to recapitulate
and refresh a latent resource of our nature: one might say
of them what Frost says of the well at the end of his poem
"Directive": "Here are your waters and your watering
place. / Drink and be whole again beyond confusion."
And so it follows that a poetry which gives access to origin
by thus embodying the lineaments of pristine speech will
fulfill, at a level below theme and intention, a definite
social function. As Marjorie Sabin has written:

Frost in 1914 wanted to believe—and wrote poems out of the belief—that human vitality takes on a supra-personal existence in the established intonations of speech . . . What Frost calls "the abstract vitality of our speech" . . . participates in the verbal forms through which other people also enact their lives.

When I fixed upon the title for this essay, I had not read Marjorie Sabin's perceptive comment (included by William Pritchard in *Robert Frost: A Literary Portrait*). But her observation about the vitality of speech taking on a supra-personal existence parallels and answers the things I am hoping to bring into focus through the phrase "above the brim."

This phrase is Frost's own and comes in that heady climbing part of "Birches"—climbing in the musical as much as in the physical sense—where he describes the boy's joyful, expert ascent toward the top of a slender birch tree. Even though the lines that conclude the poem are among some of the most familiar in the canon of twentieth-century verse, I still feel it worthwhile to quote them:

> He always kept his poise
> To the top branches, climbing carefully
> With the same pains you use to fill a cup
> Up to the brim, and even above the brim.
> Then he flung outward, feet first, with a swish,
> Kicking his way down through the air to the ground.
> So was I once myself a swinger of birches.
> And so I dream of going back to be.

It's when I'm weary of considerations,
And life is too much like a pathless wood
Where your face burns and tickles with the cobwebs
Broken across it, and one eye is weeping
From a twig's having lashed across it open.
I'd like to get away from earth awhile
And then come back to it and begin over.
May no fate willfully misunderstand me
And half grant what I wish and snatch me away
Not to return. Earth's the right place for love:
I don't know where it's likely to go better.
I'd like to go by climbing a birch tree,
And climb black branches up a snow-white trunk
Toward heaven, till the tree could bear no more,
But dipped its top and set me down again.
That would be good both going and coming back.
One could do worse than be a swinger of birches.

This seesawing between earth and heaven nicely represents the principle of redress which I have elsewhere commended. That general inclination to begin a countermove once things go too far in any given direction is enacted by "Birches" with lovely pliant grace. But my main concern here is with the specifically upward waft of Frost's poems, and the different ways in which he releases the feeling, preeminent in the lines just quoted, of airy vernal daring, an overbrimming of invention and of what he once called "supply." The sensation of lucky strike which he describes in his preface to the *Collected Poems* matches very closely the sensation of flourish and plenty which characterizes "Birches." Here are some relevant lines from "The Figure a Poem Makes":

For me the initial delight is in the surprise of remembering something I didn't know I knew . . . There is a glad recognition of the long lost and the rest follows. Step by step the wonder of unexpected supply keeps growing.

The headiness of Frost's poetry has much to do with this revel in artesian energies, as the poet plays eagerly to the top of his bent and then goes over the top and down the other side. But it is not just the sheer happiness of composition that creates a rise of poetic levels. The opposite condition, the sheer unhappiness of the uncomposed world, is even more conducive to the art of the ascending scale. When Frost comes down hard upon the facts of hurt, he still manages to end up gaining poetic altitude. As his intelligence thrusts down, it creates a reactive force capable of raising and carrying the whole burden of our knowledge and experience.

"Home Burial," for example, is a great poem which ends well above the brim of its last line. Its buoyancy is achieved in direct proportion to its pressure upon the ground of the actual. The poem derives from a cruel moment in the married life of the young Robert and Elinor Frost, when their first child, a boy not quite four, died of *cholera infantum* in 1900; and yet "Home Burial" contains no pathos, no Victorian chiaroscuro. It is one of the best of Frost's dramatic eclogues, with all the rigor and dispatch of Greek tragedy.

A husband comes upon a wife, traumatized by grief at the death of their child, keeping a trembly, furious vigil over the grave. The grave is visible through the window of their semi-isolated house, and is the locus around which their drama of recrimination and rebuke exhausts itself. Indeed, the point I want to make is that the entrapment of the couple, their feral involvement with each other as each other's quarry and companion, is not held at a safe narrative distance but interrupts into the space between reader and text. The mixture of anger, panic, and tyranny in the husband's voice at the end of the poem is rendered with a fairness and bareness that presses closure to an extreme where it virtually constitutes a reopening. The top of the reader's head is lifted like the latch of the protagonist's tormented home, and the lifting power resides in the upsurge of language. Both Randall Jarrell and Joseph Brodsky have written magnificently about the poem in line-by-line commentaries which need not be repeated here. Instead, I will quote the final lines where a premature diminuendo is fiercely contradicted. The husband seeks to clear the emotional air too soon and too proprietorially, in a move to suppress the wildness of the wife's sorrow; but when the sound of *her* sense rises in the perfectly pitched anger, he can no longer restrain the note of tyranny:

> "There, you have said it all and you feel better.
> You won't go now. You're crying. Close the door.
> The heart's gone out of it: why keep it up?
> Amy! There's someone coming down the road!"

"*You*—oh, you think the talk is all. I must go—
Somewhere out of this house. How can I make
you—"

"If—you—do!" She was opening the door wider.
"Where do you mean to go? First tell me that.
I'll follow and bring you back by force. I *will!*—"

This rising note out of the fallen condition is the
essential one which Frost achieves in his greatest work.
It is the outcry that comes when he follows his early
advice to himself, which was to lean hard upon the facts
until they hurt. It is writing which is free of Frost's usual
emotional protectiveness, and it represents the highest
level of his achievement as a poet.

To say this is not to undervalue the mellow resource
of Frost's voice at what we might call cruising altitude,
or "middle flight," as Milton called it. In that range, the
poet draws *indirectly* upon a wisdom which in his greatest
poems seems to be wrested *directly* from experience itself.
Yet this indirection of his typical level-best work is not
an evasion· within its beguiling melodies there is secluded
a strong awareness of that unbeguiling world to which
the melodies themselves offer a conscious resistance. In-
deed, a recurring theme in Frost's work is the way a
particular music can actually constitute a meaning. In
"The Oven Bird," for example, the bird has the unique
gift of knowing how in singing not to sing; and "The
question that he frames in all but words / Is what to make
of a diminished thing." On the other hand, the song of

the phoebes at the end of the poem "The Need of Being
Versed in Country Things" is so perfectly matched to
human sentiment that it must be resisted because it is a
kind of siren song. The birds come flying through the
burnt-out ruin of a deserted house, but even so:

> For them there was really nothing sad.
> But though they rejoiced in the nest they kept,
> One had to be versed in country things
> Not to believe the phoebes wept.

This mixture of the rejoicing notes and the weeping notes,
however, is exactly what Frost achieved in the sonnet
"Never Again Would Birds' Song Be the Same," which
is, among other things, an oblique dramatic statement of
his own poetic creed. What we have here is not quite an
allegory and not just an orotundity: we have that sensation
of speech in free supply, welling up and riding fluently
on the old sounds of sense, moving animatedly and skill-
fully over and back across the pattern of the verse form.
Here, too, birdsong, that most conventional of analogies
for poetic utterance, is being presented as something bear-
ing traces of prelapsarian freedom and felicity. To mis-
quote Hopkins slightly, it is the note that man was made
for. In Frost's trope, the song of the birds is tuned to the
note of Eve's voice in Eden, in much the same way as
poetry is tuned to the sound of sense, and to those tones
of voice that live in the original cave of the mouth. The
choral joys of the mythic garden and the actual resource

of the vocal cords are harmonized within a wonderful, seemingly effortless heft of language:

> He would declare and could himself believe
> That the birds there in all the garden round
> From having heard the daylong voice of Eve
> Had added to their own an oversound,
> Her tone of meaning but without the words.
> Admittedly an eloquence so soft
> Could only have had an influence on birds
> When call or laughter carried it aloft.
> Be that as may be, she was in their song.
> Moreover her voice upon their voices crossed
> Had now persisted in the woods so long
> That probably it never would be lost.
> Never again would birds' song be the same.
> And to do that to birds was why she came.

"He would declare and could himself believe": The first line is in the conditional, optative mood, so all that follows has to be conditional and in part wishful. There is a lovely certitude in the fantasy, but there is a regretful understanding that it is indeed a fantasy; so there is a counterweight in the line "Never again would birds' song be the same" that works against the poem's logical sense. The poem's argument, as I read it, ought to lead to the conclusion that the changed note of the birds' song should be an occasion of joy, since it happened in Paradise and was effected by the paradisial voice of Eve. But that logic is complicated by the actual note of repining that we hear

in the line "Never again would birds' song be the same,"
a note that comes from the fact that we are now beyond
Eden, at a great distance of time and space. The Adam
figure, the "he" of the poem, has suffered exile from his
prelapsarian bliss, so there is a counterweight of heart-
break in the statement of what seemed in the beginning
a heart-lifting truth.

Memories of Eden-like joys corrected and countered
by an acknowledgment of their inevitable passing also
underlie Frost's poem "To Earthward." This poem takes
us back to Frost at his very strongest. It belongs with
"Home Burial," but is intensely lyrical rather than starkly
dramatic. The quatrains are like fossils, constrained
within their shapes but minutely and energetically ex-
pressive of the life that gave them shape:

> Love at the lips was touch
> As sweet as I could bear;
> And once that seemed too much;
> I lived on air
>
> That crossed me from sweet things,
> The flow of—was it musk
> From hidden grapevine springs
> Down hill at dusk?
>
> I had the swirl and ache
> From sprays of honeysuckle
> That when they're gathered shake
> Dew on the knuckle.

I craved strong sweets, but those
Seemed strong when I was young;
The petal of the rose
It was that stung.

Now no joy but lacks salt
That is not dashed with pain
And weariness and fault;
I crave the stain

Of tears, the aftermark
Of almost too much love,
The sweet of bitter bark
And burning clove.

When stiff and sore and scarred
I take away my hand
From leaning on it hard
In grass and sand,

The hurt is not enough:
I long for weight and strength
To feel the earth as rough
To all my length.

This poem goes from living and walking on air to living and enduring on earth. It redresses the motion of "Birches," in which the boy climbed in order to be set down. Here the man is sustained even as he seeks to descend. The more he submits himself to the drag of experience and the pull of some moral g-factor, the more a reactive thrust is generated against it. The poetic situation at the end of "To Earthward" is rather different from the pictorial one. Pictorially, we are offered an image of the body hugging the earth, seeking to penetrate to the very *humus* in humility, wishing the ground were a penitential bed. But the paradoxical result of this drive toward abasement is a marvel of levitation: in spite of the physical push to earthward, the psychic direction is skyward. The state of things at the end of the poem is something like that formulated at the end of Frost's sonnet "A Soldier," which deals with the old subject of patriotic death in battle through a beautifully turned conceit. The soldier's body is like a lance in the dust, fallen from its trajectory. Even so, consolation can be found:

> But this we know, the obstacle that checked
> And tripped the body, shot the spirit on
> Further than target ever showed or shone.

The sensation of spirit not so much projected onward as brimming over and above the body is what is thrilling in "To Earthward." There is a wonderful, supple, uningratiating presentation of self going on. The poem does not say "I have faults and deserve to be punished," although it may ruefully admit to this if we put the words in its mouth. Nor does it say "What a good boy am I, to be so grown up at last." Frost is not running for cover behind cocksureness or blandishment, nor is he exercising that verbal sleight of hand which sometimes furnishes too nifty resolutions to other poems. What this poem advances is all guaranteed. It is neither specter nor sculpture: cut this verse and it will bleed. Compare it, for example, with an equivalent poem by Yeats, "Men Improve with the Years," and you are faced with something unexpected: Frost's is the poem in which he walks naked, Yeats's the one which appears more ironical and protected. The warmth of wanting to feel the earth "as rough / To all my length" contrasts well with Yeats's project of coldness in "Men Improve with the Years":

> But I grow old among dreams,
> A weather-worn, marble triton
> Among the streams.

To emphasize this recurring pattern is to highlight something of distinctive and durable value in Frost's work. It does seem to me that the poems which hold up most strongly embody one or the other of the following movements: a movement which consists of or is analogous to a fullness overflowing, or the corollary of that, a kind of reactive wave, a fullness in the process of rebounding off something or somebody else.

For examples of a fullness overflowing without complication, we need to look no further than his first collection, A Boy's Will, where the two acknowledged triumphs are "The Tuft of Flowers" and "Mowing." After all, the flowers which are the occasion of the former poem owe their very survival to what Frost calls "sheer morning gladness at the brim," a gladness which inspired the mower to spare them and so, by a little chain reaction of rapture, inspired the poem. Furthermore, in the sonnet about mowing, where the heart of the poetic matter is the whisper of the scythe, that scythe-whisper is itself presented as a welling up of something out of silence, an expression almost of the silence's own abounding relish of itself:

> There was never a sound beside the wood but one,
> And that was my long scythe whispering to the ground.
> What was it it whispered? I knew not well myself;
> Perhaps it was something about the heat of the sun,
> Something, perhaps, about the lack of sound—
> And that was why it whispered and did not speak.
> It was no dream of the gift of idle hours,
> Or easy gold at the hand of fay or elf:
> Anything more than the truth would have seemed too
> weak
> To the earnest love that laid the swale in rows,
> Not without feeble-pointed spikes of flowers
> (Pale orchises), and scared a bright green snake.
> The fact is the sweetest dream that labor knows.
> My long scythe whispered and left the hay to make.

This early poem broadcasts a sweetness that we credit easily and that we should set in the balance against the tales of the old poet's vanity and vindictiveness. Its melodies possess a wonderful justifying force, and remind us that Frost is, among other things, one of the most irresistible masters of the sonnet in the English language.

(Think of the overbrimming technical joys of "The Silken Tent" or the high tides of mutuality in "Meeting and Passing.")

And yet, the bleaker the recognitions being forced upon Frost, the greater the chance of the absolute poem. I am thinking of a work such as "An Old Man's Winter Night," which expresses what I earlier called "the crystal of indifference" at the core of Frost's being, that which takes in and gives back the signals of a universal solitude. Samuel Beckett would surely incline an appreciative ear to the following lines, where the figure of age, in all its factuality and loneliness, is plainly and strangely rendered:

> He stood with barrels round him—at a loss.
> And having scared the cellar under him
> In clomping here, he scared it once again
> In clomping off;— and scared the outer night,
> Which has its sounds, familiar, like the roar
> Of trees and crack of branches, common things,
> But nothing so like beating on a box.
> A light he was to no one but himself
> Where now he sat, concerned with he knew what,
> A quiet light, and then not even that.

To read lines like these is to apprehend fleetingly what Frost means by his compelling if enigmatic declaration in "Mowing" that "The fact is the sweetest dream that labor knows." It certainly would seem that he intends this to be more than a plea for writing as a form of

85

documentary realism. Even though such realism was what Ezra Pound found praiseworthy when he reviewed *North of Boston*—"Mr. Frost's people are real people"—and even though it contributed vividly to my own original pleasure in his work, it is not what the final sweetest dream is about.

In the beginning, however, I did love coming upon the inner evidence of Frost's credentials as a farmer poet. I admired, for example, the way he could describe (in "The Code") how forkfuls of hay were built upon a wagonload for easy unloading later, when they have to be tossed down from underfoot. And sometimes the evidence was more general but still completely credible, such as that fiercely direct account of a child's hand being cut off by a circular saw and the child's sudden simple death. Coming as I did from a world of farmyard stories about men crushed in quarry machinery or pulled into the drums of threshing mills, I recognized the note of grim accuracy in the poem called "Out, Out—." I was immediately susceptible to its documentary weight and did not mistake the wintry report of what happened at the end for the poet's own callousness.

Nevertheless, the counterweight, the oversound, the sweetest dream within the fact—these things are poetically more rewarding than a record, however faithful, of the data. This is why the imagined hardness of "The Most of It" more than holds its own against the cruel reporting of "Out, Out—," why the extravagance of "The Witch of Coös" excels the pastoral of "The Ax-Helve," and why the mysteriously intuited happenings at

the end of "Two Look at Two" are more sustaining than
the nostalgic wishfulness in the last line of "Directive":

> Two had seen two, whichever side you spoke from.
> "This *must* be all." It was all. Still they stood,
> A great wave from it going over them,
> As if the earth in one unlooked-for favor
> Had made them certain earth returned their love.

At such moments, and in such poems—if I may repeat
my notion one last time—a fullness rebounds back upon
itself, or it rebounds off something or someone else and
thereby creates a wave capable of lifting the burden of
our knowledge and the experience to a new, refreshing
plane. Moreover, this bracing lyric power is as dependent
on Frost's sense of his own faults as it is on his faultless
ear. Implicit in many of the poems I have been praising
is a capacity to recognize the shortcomings in himself,
and to judge himself for the shortfall between his life and
his art. But what is implicit in the poems is explicit in a
dialogue which Robert Lowell records and which I wish
to quote in conclusion. Here, from Lowell's collection
History, is part of the sonnet which he calls plainly "Rob-
ert Frost":

> Robert Frost at midnight, the audience gone
> to vapor, the great act laid on the shelf in mothballs,
> his voice is musical and raw—he writes in the flyleaf:
> *For Robert from Robert, his friend in the art.*
> "Sometimes I feel too full of myself," I say.

And he, misunderstanding, "When I am low,
I stray away . . ."

[. . .]

And I, "Sometimes I'm so happy I can't stand myself."
And he, "When I am too full of joy, I think
how little good my health did anyone near me."

1990

DEREK WALCOTT

The Road Taken

Robert Frost being interviewed at the University of Detroit,
November 13, 1962. (From the collection of Peter Stanlis)

On that gusting day of the inauguration of the young emperor, the sublime Augustan moment of a country that was not just a republic but also an empire, no more a homespun vision of pioneer values but a world power, no figure was more suited to the ceremony than Robert Frost. He had composed a poem for the occasion, but he could not read it in the glare and the wind, so instead he recited one that many had heard and perhaps learned by heart.

> The land was ours before we were the land's.
> She was our land more than a hundred years
> Before we were her people.

This was the calm reassurance of American destiny that provoked Tonto's response to the Lone Ranger. No slavery, no colonization of Native Americans, a process of dispossession and then possession, but nothing about the dispossession of others that this destiny demanded. The choice of poem was not visionary so much as defensive. A Navajo hymn might have been more appropriate: the "ours" and the "we" of Frost were not as ample and multihued as Whitman's tapestry, but something as tight and regional as a Grandma Moses painting, a Currier and Ives print, strictly New England in black and white.

By then as much an emblem of the republic as any rubicund senator with his flying white hair, an endangered species like a rare owl, there was the old poet who, between managing the fluttering white hair and the fluttering white paper, had to recite what sounded more like an elegy than a benediction. "The land was ours before we were the land's" could have had no other name, not only because he was then in his old age, but because all his spirit and career, like Thomas Hardy's, lurched toward a wintry wisdom.

·

Robert Frost: the icon of Yankee values, the smell of wood smoke, the sparkle of dew, the reality of farmhouse dung, the jocular honesty of an uncle.

Why is the favorite figure of American patriotism not paternal but avuncular? Because uncles are wiser than fathers. They have humor, they keep their distance, they are bachelors, they can't be fooled by rhetoric. Frost loved playing the uncle, relishing the dry enchantment of his own voice, the homely gravel in the throat, the keep-your-distance pseudo-rusticity that suspected every stranger, meaning every reader. The voice is like its weather. It tells you to stay away until you are invited. Its first lines, in the epigraph to Frost's 1949 *Complete Poems*, are not so much invitations as warnings.

> I'm going out to clean the pasture spring;
> I'll only stop to rake the leaves away
> (And wait to watch the water clear, I may):
> I sha'n't be gone long.—You come too.

From the very epigraph, then, the surly ambiguities slide in. Why "I may"? Not for the rhyme, the desperation of doggerel, but because of this truth: that it would take too long to watch the agitated clouded water settle, that is, for as long as patience allows the poet to proceed to the next line. (Note that the parentheses function as a kind of container, or bank, or vessel, of the churned spring.) The refrain, "You come too." An invitation? An order? And how sincere is either? That is the point of Frost's tone, the authoritative but ambiguous distance of a master ironist.

Frost is an autocratic poet rather than a democratic poet. His invitations are close-lipped, wry, quiet; neither the voice nor the metrical line has the open-armed municipal mural expansion of the other democratic poet, Whitman. The people in Frost's dramas occupy a tight and taciturn locale. They are not part of Whitman's parade of blacksmiths, wheelwrights made communal by work. Besieged and threatened, their virtues are as cautious and measured as the scansion by which they are portrayed.

Many of the uncollected poems in the Library of America's *Robert Frost: Collected Poems, Prose, and Plays* are negligible, but only because they pale beside the triumph of the best and familiar Frost. They neither add to nor detract from the reputation. There is a hefty representation of them, and like all the famous whose every fragment is hoarded by the academy, Frost has to pay for his fame with certain embarrassments, such as this verse from 1890:

> The 'tzin quick springeth to his side,
> His mace he hurls on high,
> It crasheth through the Spanish steel,
> And Leon prone doth lie.

and:

> When I was young, we dwelt in a vale
> By a misty fen that rang all night,
> And thus it was the maidens pale . . .

Through the Wordsworthian vocabulary of "Upon each grove and mead," to the ambulatory reflection on the pastoral sublime, the evolving Frost is predictable, dutiful as the early Keats is to Milton, to what is expected of the nature poet. First, there is the generic blur, and then, as in John Clare, the haze lifts and leaf and stone are magnified in detail like grass after a rain shower. We rattle the box for gems among the dud stones and find "Genealogical" and "The Middletown Murder" and this early

one (c. 1890s) which is equal in steadiness to middle
Frost:

> The reason of my perfect ease
> In the society of trees
> Is that their cruel struggles pass
> Too far below my social class
> For me to share them or be made
> For what I am and love afraid.

And there is the early debt to Hardy:

> Those stones out under the low-limbed tree
> Doubtless bear names that the mosses mar.

.

By technical convention and even in tone, the poet
of A Boy's Will is an English poet, not a New England
poet, an exiled Georgian, already skillful in the springing
resilience of his verses and the measured plot of harmony
and homily in their stanzas. There are signs of that cun-
ning of adaptation, of seizure, that great poets show in
their ambition, the way Eliot shamelessly raided La-
forgue; and so we can watch Frost stalking Hardy through
shadowy woods, keeping his own distance, but measuring
his own hesitancy until he takes his own road, which will
diverge from Hardy and the English pastoralists, and hits
his own stride, this jocular stride of the open road ap-
parent in W. H. Davies, in Whitman, in "Two Tramps
in Mud Time."

In 1912, when he was thirty-eight, Frost left Boston with his family for England, to devote himself to writing. He submitted *A Boy's Will*, his first collection, to the English publisher David Nutt, and it was accepted. He lived in a cottage in Buckinghamshire. In London, at Harold Munro's Poetry Bookshop, he met the poet F. S. Flint, who introduced him to Ezra Pound. Pound gave *A Boy's Will* a good review because, for all his aggressive cosmopolitanism and campaigning for the classics and "the new," Pound was as much a vernacular regional poet as Frost, and the genuine Americanness of Frost must have stirred a patriotic claim in him as much as the tonal authenticity of Eliot did. He derided the falsely modern and saw a classic shape in Frost that made "it" (poetry) new by its directness and its vigor: Frost's writing achieved a vernacular elation in tone, not with the cheap device of dialect spelling or rustic vocabulary, but with a clean ear and a fresh eye. (Pound found the same qualities in Hemingway.) And Yeats told Pound that *A Boy's Will* was "the best poetry written in America for a long time." The judgment remains right.

It was in England, in discussions with Flint and T. E. Hulme, that Frost clarified his direction by "the sounds of sense with all their irregularity of accent across the regular beat of the metre." Pound's encouragement —or, better, his papal benediction—turned into belligerence. Frost calls Pound a "quasi-friend" and writes: "He says I must write something much more like *vers libre* or he will let me perish by neglect. He really threatens." He worries that Pound's good review of *North of*

Boston will describe him as one of Pound's "party of American literary refugees." (Later, down the years, down their different roads, Frost petitioned against Pound's imprisonment, even if he was enraged at the award of the Bollingen Prize to him; and Pound himself had no choice but to recognize the syntactical variety in Frost's verse, the *vers libre* within the taut frame.)

•

Frost's early mastery of stress looks natural. A deftness, like a skipping stone, evades the predictable scansion by a sudden parenthesis, by a momentarily forgotten verb—"that laid the swale in rows . . . and scared a bright green snake," and shifting, dancing caesuras.

> Anything more than the truth would have seemed too
> weak
> To the earnest love that laid the swale in rows,
> Not without feeble-pointed spikes of flowers
> (Pale orchises), and scared a bright green snake.

Yet the dialogue of the dramatic poems is boxed in by a metrical rigidity that, strangely enough, is more stiff-backed than the narration, perhaps because these poems are thought of as one element of the whole poem rather than as theater, where narration recedes in the presence of action and the variety of individual voices solidifies the contradictions of melody character by character. "The Death of the Hired Man" and others are poems, and not plays, for this reason: the voice of the characters and their creator is one voice, Frost's, and one tone, something nearer to complaint and elegy than vocal conflict, the tragic edge instead of tragedy. It's as if all his characters were remembering poems by Robert Frost. From "A Hundred Collars":

> "It's business, but I can't say it's not fun.
> What I like best's the lay of different farms,
> Coming out on them from a stretch of woods,
> Or over a hill or round a sudden corner.
> I like to find folks getting out in spring,
> Raking the dooryard, working near the house."

.

A certain deadening of the ear had dated dramatic verse since the Victorians, who tried to resuscitate Elizabethan and Jacobean drama through the pentameter, prolonging a hollow, martial echo that could not render the ordinary and domestic, that did not take into account the charged and broken syntax of Webster or the late Shakespeare. The same reverential monody occurred in Victorian epic poetry. The Elizabethan echo had become part of the soaring architecture, a determination to be sublime that again divided the lyric from the dramatic voice, that took poetry away from the theater and back into the library. Frost felt that in New England he was being offered an unexplored, unuttered theater, away from the leaves of libraries, in a natural setting rich with stories and characters.

We think of Frost's work in theatrical terms, with

the poet, of course, as its central character, mocking his crises, his stopping at a crossroads, but also because of the voices in the poems. These voices are American, but their meter is not as subtly varied as the lyrical and yet colloquial power of his own meditations. To read the "Masques," at least for this reader, is a duty, not a delight. One keeps wishing that they were plays, not theatrical poems. The vocabulary grows ornate:

> The myrrh tree gives it. Smell the rosin burning?
> The ornaments the Greek artificers
> Made for the Emperor Alexius . . .
> [. . .]
> And hark, the gold enameled nightingales
> Are singing.

The line is sometimes unspeakable:

> You poor, poor swallowable little man.

The humor is arch:

> Job: But, yes, I'm fine, except for now and then
> A reminiscent twinge of rheumatism.

"Vulgarity," the gift that comes from the mob, which great poetic dramatists possess, no matter how sublime their rhetoric, and which they need in order to force a single response from an audience, springs from the vernacular, from the oral rather than the written, and is based on popular banalities of humor and pathos—this power is what separates, say, Browning from Shakespeare, this eagerness to entertain, to put it crassly. With his own gifts of the vernacular and of self-dramatization, Frost might be expected to have produced a wide, popular theater, since the tone of American speech was ready and resolved. And yet, for all his winking and his intimacy, Frost is a very private poet.

When we imagine the single voice of Frost behind the lines, it is the sound of a personal vernacular, but heard as dialogue. The vernacular petrifies into the monodic, perhaps because the dramatic poem (is there a single really successful example in literature?) is a kind of mule, like the prose poem, and like the "Masques." The contradiction of any masque is the pitch of its diction; it is meant not to be acted but to be heard. Frost's theatrical dialogue has a monodic drone. Yeats, who in the beginning of his theatrical career was as dutiful to the pentameter as Frost remained, finally broke away from it vehemently and triumphantly in "Purgatory," and he did so with a rapid and common diction that came from the pub and the street, until the lyric and dramatic pitch were one sound, as it is with the Jacobeans. In Frost's poetical theater, the diction becomes stately, working almost against the accent. It was not a betrayal or a defeat but a matter of temperament. Frost's temperament was too hermetic for the theater.

·

But something wonderful, revolutionary within the convention, happened to Frost's ear between *A Boy's Will* and *North of Boston*. He wrote American, without vehement challenge. He wrote free or syllabic verse within the deceptive margins of the pentameter. He played tennis, to use his famous description, but you couldn't see the net; his caesuras slid with a wry snarl over the surface, over the apparently conventional scansion.

> Something there is that doesn't love a wall . . .

appears, to eye and ear, to be:

> Some / thing / there is / that doesn't / love / a wall . . .

That is certainly how it would sound in English, to the Georgian ear. But think American. In that diction, parody is the basis of pronunciation, and there is only one caesura:

> Something there is / that doesn't love a wall . .

That rapid elision or slur of the second half of the line is as monumental a breakthrough for American verse as any experiment by Williams or Cummings. It dislocates the pivot of traditional scansion; and the consequence is seismic but inimitable, because it is first of all Frost's voice, which in meter is first regional, then generic, eventually American. This happened with equal force to

Yeats, but with Frost it is more alarming, since Yeats contracted the pentameter to octosyllabics for propulsion's sake, for "that quarrel with others which we call rhetoric," for the purposes of political passion, but Frost achieved this upheaval within the pentameter. He accomplished it, that is, without making his meter as wry and sarcastic as Williams's, or as pyrotechnic as Cummings's, or as solemn and portentous as Stevens's.

.

Once that confidence sprung to hand and voice, there was no other road for Frost but greatness, a greatness not of ambition but of vocation:

> Two roads diverged in a yellow wood,
> And sorry I could not travel both
> And be one traveler . . .

I am quoting from memory, which is the greatest tribute to poetry, and with some strain I could probably copy from the dictation of memory not only this poem but also several other poems of Frost's. For interior recitation, usually of complete poems, not only of lines or stanzas, Frost and Yeats, for their rhythm and design, are the most memorable poets of the century.

To fight against a predictable tone of incantation was a great task for the American. Yeats could ride the lilt and history of a long tradition. Frost was truly alone, and many of the poems dramatize his own singularity—not the romantic image of the neglected poet in a materialist society but the American romance of the pioneer, the inventor, the tinkerer (if the pentameter wasn't broken, why fix it?), who knows the rational needs of that society, one of which is the practicality of poetry, its workday occupation, the fusion of commerce and art, of carpentry and metrical composition, the "song of the open road." Whitman's vagabondage is romantic, perhaps even irresponsible. Frost stays put, close to stone walls, under apple orchards, mowing grass, his view of the republic a blue haze of hills, rigidly Horatian.

> There was never a sound beside the wood but one,
> And that was my long scythe whispering to the ground.

In formal verse, tension creates memory, the taut lines between the poles of the margins, and shape is as much a cause of that tension as stanzas and their breathing spaces, also carefully measured between the stanza patterns. Stanzaic structure creates anticipation; and the verbal music, by its chords, its elisions, its caesuras, delights the ear when expectation is confirmed, but with additional surprise. This is the masterly delight of Dickinson, "the slant of light," her assonant obliquities in slant rhymes. But this is a technique which Frost rarely uses. His rhymes are rich and unsurprising; it is their thought, their argument, what he calls "reason," that delights us. The tension that we enjoy in Frost is that of another slant or viewpoint at what was once ordinary, its melodious sarcasm.

> Now I am old my teachers are the young.
> What can't be molded must be cracked and sprung.
> I strain at lessons fit to start a suture.
> I go to school to youth to learn the future.

North of Boston consists of monologues and narrative pieces, dialogues in a fixed landscape, with its subterranean terror of madness as in "A Servant to Servants," destitution in "The Death of the Hired Man," black humor in "Blueberries," infant mortality in "Home Burial," and, best of all, "The Fear." But the metronomic rhythm of their dialogue, the inflexible morality, these pinched tragedies in which their narrow lives are seeped, can tire attention. Something mean, sour, and embittered, like the late mulch of November soil, rises from the pages and disturbs us with the kind of punishment that a tireless gossip demands of his hearer. This is a mercilessly moral climate that produces attic idiots and witch-hunters.

It terrifies the outsider in its eccentric smugness; but this may be the legendary severity of the North as surely as a lyric mania and a corrupt languor are the legendary climate of the South. (From Frost to Faulkner.) With *Mountain Interval*, the lyric freshness of the temperature of a brook in spring pours with the usual clarity over its stone nouns. Or, like cows homing at dusk for the barns, they head for the open door of anthologies—"Two Tramps in Mud Time," "An Old Man's Winter Night," "The Oven Bird," "Birches"—slapped on their haunches to ruminate in their fragrant stalls.

Frost is Whitman's heir in the magnification of close

domestic objects and creatures, the "noiseless, patient spider" of his writing hand, a Protestant quality, pragmatic and commonplace as a Dutch interior, the "slant of light" that his other progenitrix, Dickinson, contemplated. The same slant that requires the imagination to honor and to record the oblique, as the great Dutch kitchen painters did, came naturally to Frost's sense of composition and balance. The "slant of light" is also a figure of irregular scansion within the frame of the window of the poem, in which the human subject is stilled by the angled light into vacancy and reflection.

Fall approaches, and with the fall, the poetry of Frost, not so much in full flare like the harlequinade of Stevens, but early and late fall, the line or branch of the verse with tentative colors, then the words dropping naturally off the lines into a heap at the base of the poem's column; the mood of "bare ruined choirs," of "My November Guest." That strain of melancholy, so self-posturing in its easy metaphor unless it is dominated by an imagination that defies it, is the interior weather that Frost divined in Edward Thomas, whom he met in England and for whom he became an example and an inspiration. Frost heard the true quiet of sorrow that gleamed under Thomas's prose, a power of meditation that did not use lyricism for spiritual release but for even more unrelenting questions. Frost saw in Thomas another kind of grace, a knightly, doomed demeanor and an alarming simplicity of courage. All his gift needed was a gentle nudging into meter.

Thomas's poems are not minor Frost, and Frost

would not have encouraged Thomas to write verse that was only an English rendition of his voice. He could not make an echo of the Englishman because their accents were different, and accent is scansion. Frost was closer to Georgian pastoral than Thomas could ever be to Frost's vernacular. The differences appear superficial, but they are deep. They have their particularities of posture and temperament: Frost belligerently assured, impatient with sadness, Thomas querulous and haunted by an unshakable melancholy; the American full of aphorism and zest, the Englishman carrying a taciturn foreshadowing of his country's pastoral decline, a lament that leads us to Larkin's "And that will be England gone." Tears prickle at the openheartedness of Thomas's bewilderment, his spiritual and syntactical hesitations. We owe to Frost the existence of Edward Thomas's pure poetry. An act of immortal generosity.

We are amazed at the ordinariness, even the banality, of Frost's rhymes ("bird," / "heard"), at the courage, even the gall, of the poet, rubbing such worn-out coins again but somehow polishing them to a surprising sheen. This directness has danger in it, the same danger it had for Wordsworth in *Lyrical Ballads*; and that sensation of danger is the ground of Frost's technical courage, and our pleasure in its smiling triumph. The slant or half rhymes of great practitioners such as Dickinson or Wilfred Owen are muted pyrotechnics; they startle, and dislocate, anticipation. But Frost's power lies in the ease with which he slides over his endings with the calm, natural authority of a wave or a gust of wind, making his rhymes, with

apparent diffidence, a part of the elements, of poetry and
of weather.

.

America likes its sages ordinary but reclusive, and
without sexual passion or desire of any kind, as much as
it likes them—Dickinson, Jeffers, Frost, Hopper—cyn-
ical of material progress, and the more cynical the more
revered. Frost's image became one of a man whittling
near an iron stove in a small country store. He played
the cynical American Horace as carefully as any sophis-
ticated celebrity or rough politician, his clauses like curled
shavings, dry, crisp, and parenthetical. Sometimes the
wisdom can be vexing in its parochialism. Frost was the
true opposite of that other sage, Robinson Jeffers. Here,
indeed, were two avuncular recluses, outdoor figures,
both opposed to Dickinson's confines, or caves, of parlor
and chapel, one on the Pacific coast and the other on
the Atlantic coast, both proffering rocky, granite-featured
profiles to "the elements," one the companion of seals
and spray, the other of deer and birds. They are stone
heads of reassuring integrity, until we look more closely
and see how frightening the cracks are in their classic,
petrified composure, how alarming and even treacherous
are their ambiguities of crossing shadows.
    Jeffers's long line, like a wave gathering and break-
ing, is already an inevitable self-evident truth, a meter
that gathers its reflection to break and shudder the sup-
posed solidity of the shore of the republic, carrying gar-
bage in its wash sometimes, and obviously, admirably

striving to achieve distance, not through any subtle domestic irritations but through the sarcasm of rage, from the hawk-height of the sublime coasting on its own serenity. This is almost a barren severity, like the rock coast that his meter celebrates, the diction already Sophoclean without the labor and the complexity, and utterly wanting in the vernacular humor that exists in all great poets, the raw peculiarity, even provinciality of Dante, Shakespeare, and the always-colloquial Frost. The diction of Jeffers is the stillborn sublime, the majestic tone that he considers fit for a stupendous and humbling coastline. The cracks in the stone are treated as tragic flaws, not as common mistakes.

.

A parody of Frost, on the other hand, would use the doggerel of the greeting card. The trap is the poem, which snaps back at us and catches our fingers with the slow revelation of its betraying our sing-along into wisdom. Frost said it with less venom: "A poem begins in delight and ends in wisdom." This leaves out the turmoil, contradictions, and anguish of the process, the middle of the journey.

> Whose woods these are I think I know.
> His house is in the village though;
> He will not see me stopping here
> To watch his woods fill up with snow.

My little horse must think it queer
To stop without a farmhouse near
Between the woods and frozen lake
The darkest evening of the year.

He gives his harness bells a shake
To ask if there is some mistake.
The only other sound's the sweep
Of easy wind and downy flake.

The woods are lovely, dark and deep,
But I have promises to keep,
And miles to go before I sleep,
And miles to go before I sleep.

And even this poem, we now know, cannot be
trusted. "Whose woods these are I think I know." He
does know, so why the hesitancy? Certainly, by the end
of the line, he has a pretty good guess. No, the subject
is not the ownership of the woods, the legal name of their
proprietor, it is the fear of naming the woods, of the
anthropomorphic heresy or the hubris of possession by
owners and poets.

The next line, generally read as an intoned filler for
the rhymes, and also praised for the regionality of that
"though" as being very American, is a daring, superflu-
ous, and muted parenthesis. "His house is in the village
though." Why not? Why shouldn't he live in the woods?
What is he scared of? Of possession, of the darkness of

the world in the woods, from his safe world of light and known, named things. He's lucky, the frightened poem says, while I'm out here in the dark evening with the first flakes of snow beginning to blur my vision and causing my horse to shudder, shake its reins, and ask why we have stopped. The poem darkens with terror in every homily.

.

The selection of letters in the Library of America edition is rewarding, but the letters are generally demure, even reticent. There is a crucial letter, however, to Lesley Frost Francis, in 1934, regarding conflicts of technique. This is the letter with the famous dictum about tennis without a net, but it is inevitable that we come across this sort of thing:

I read that negroes were chosen to sing her opera [Gertrude Stein's] because they have less need than white men to know what they are talking about. That is a thing that can be reported without malice.

Encountering this remark in the poet's letter to his daughter, does one sidestep it as a turd in the road, or shrug it off, or condemn its author and his time, but without the shock of insult, for what else is the remark if not American? One doesn't go ravaging the privacy of family correspondence for proof of racism, and in these dangerous times, when any group can scream injury and

litigate against the dead, sue History, and demand com-
pensation, the sudden encounter of Frost as a racist
should be neither sudden nor shocking but normal for a
white New England poet, which is how he suddenly
forces the reader of this remark to think of him. But the
passage is hardly without a lasting effect. It does some-
thing, from now on, or at least for a while, to this reader's
delight in Frost, a delight that may now be damaged,
owing to the comprehensive honesty of this book. As one
stares vacantly away from the open book, one arrives at
that moment in the *Inferno* in which the poet concludes:
"that day we read no further."

And yet we must read further, especially with Amer-
ican masters. We must read as far as the white whale
draws us, beyond the tight, calendar hamlets and
harbors of New England and its chapels with their har-
poon spires, to a wider and more terrifying space, the
elemental ocean, beyond provinciality, history, race, be-
yond America, beyond the sick anti-Semitic provincial-
ities of Pound or the patriotic regionalism of Frost to a
realm that only genius can depict. We must follow Moby
Dick, the huge ribbed metaphor of the white whale car-
rying the freight of the republic's sins as the republic
perishes in the whirlpool with a sole survivor, Melville-
Ishmael, who is, despite Melville's convictions of racial
superiority, a poet. Now that other races and other causes
in the babel of the republic have been given permission
to speak in the very language that ruled and defined them,
must everything be revised by the new order? Does Frost's

ironic, jocular accent not apply to them? But it does, because the new order would be repeating the old order if it made a policy of exclusion and an aesthetics of revenge.

.

Pound's poetry does not absolve Pound, any more than a single phrase from a letter by Frost damns Frost forever. One groans or shudders, but one pushes on. Poetry is its own realm and does not pardon. There is nothing to forgive Frost's poetry for. There are, instead, many poems to be grateful for, so many poems, indeed, that the man, the biography, the symbol of Yankee resilience are all negligible, since poetry pronounces benediction not on the poet but on the reader. A great poem is a state of raceless, sexless, timeless grace, and this book, which contains more than just a life, is too full of such benedictions for this reader not to pick it up and continue.

Skimming a great poet's life, we pause when some fact darkens and jolts the rate of the summary, clouding the passage, and we seize on something historical that corroborates a poem. But this is the wrong way to read a poem *and* a life. We know that Frost once walked all night through a swamp and transformed this into those poems of natural terror; and we know he had terrible stomach cramps as a child, that his father was an alcoholic, that "Provide, Provide" ("Too many fall from great and good / For you to doubt the likelihood") must have been owed to the terror of destitution following the cost of burying his father when $8 was all his mother was left with, which was the circumstance that brought them East, from Pacific to Atlantic, to Lawrence, Massachusetts, and made Frost a naturalized Yankee. But there is a difference between a poem and a journal. The poems essentialize the life. The poem does not obey linear time; it is, by its belligerence or its surrender, the enemy of time; and it is, when it is true, time's conqueror, not time's servant.

The much-honored Frost fought his own petrifaction into a monument by dry, didactic humor, but he could not avoid being cherished, and the self-dismissal and wryness became a part of the act, even the melancholy. "Play melancholy autumn," his readers demanded, and however chilling the tone, the audiences roared like autumn leaves around the snow haired figure behind the lectern, and the doctorates were showered on him, and the Pulitzers, and a tribute from the Senate on his seventy-fifth birthday. He wrote in "Birches":

> I'd like to get away from earth awhile
> And then come back to it and begin over.
> May no fate willfully misunderstand me
> And half grant what I wish and snatch me away
> Not to return.

He himself grew to resemble a bent birch, its flecked bark, its hoarse, whispering words. And he got away. He died, at the age of eighty-eight, in 1963, more of an emblem than any American poet except Whitman, having become decades earlier that pitted, apple-cheeked, snow-crested image that the country idealized in its elders, public and private, bucolic and cosmopolitan, avuncular and responsible. But the companionable and masterful Library of America collection proves that he has also remained. Here is the canonical Frost (which, in its gathering of Frost's lectures, essays, and stories, shows also that he wrote great fictional prose) devotedly and richly presented by Richard Poirier and Mark Richardson in a clear and airy format that lets the print breathe and echoes that easily parodied voice, quirky in its delights but certain of its calling.

> And then there was a wall of trees with trunks;
> After that only the tops of trees, and cliffs
> Imperfectly concealed among the leaves.
> A dry ravine emerged from under boughs
> Into the pasture.

A widower with a suicidal son who eventually succeeded in killing himself, Frost showed the scars of his devastations in his scansion, but they did not break his meter or pitch it into a rant that broke its disciplined confinement, for the confinement brought the discipline that his sorrow needed, nor did they abrupt it into cryptic, embittered phrases. It is perhaps this steadiness, which lasted a lifetime, that was responsible for his reputation for coldness. It was not that poetry was all that mattered, was all that he had, that made him seem cruel, but that he could close it tight in its frame like a door against foul weather, or light it, like an old lamp, against even worse weather, the black gusts that shook his soul.

1995